W9-AKV-069

George Bernard Shaw

ON LANGUAGE

GEORGE BERNARD SHAW ON LANGUAGE

Edited, with an Introduction and Notes, by
ABRAHAM TAUBER, PH. D.
Dean, Bronx Community College
The City University of New York
(Visiting Professor of Speech, Yeshiva University)

Foreword by
SIR JAMES PITMAN, K. B. E., M. P.
International authority on Shaw and alphabet and spelling reform

PHILOSOPHICAL LIBRARY
New York

 Library of Congress Catalog Card No. 63-13483. Printed in the United States of America.

DEDICATION

To Rhea, whose patient encouragement and gentle forbearance helped to bring this work to fruition.

FOREWORD

by Sir James Pitman

"I got a clue to my real condition from a friend of mine, a physician who had devoted himself specially to ophthalmic surgery. He tested my eyesight one evening, and informed me that it was quite uninteresting to him because it was normal. I naturally took this to mean that it was like everybody else's; but he rejected this construction as paradoxical, and hastened to explain to me that I was an exceptional and highly fortunate person optically, normal sight conferring the power of seeing things accurately, and being enjoyed by only about ten per cent of the population, the remaining ninety per cent being abnormal. I immediately perceived the explanation of my want of success in fiction. My mind's eye, like my body's, was 'normal': it saw things differently from other people's eyes, and saw them better.

"This revelation produced a considerable effect on me. At first it struck me that I might live by selling my works to the ten per cent who were like myself; but a moment's reflection showed me that these must all be as penniless as I, and that we could not live by taking in one another's literary washing. How to earn daily bread by my pen was then the problem. Had I been a practical commonsense moneyloving Englishman, the matter would have been easy enough: I should have put on a pair of abnormal spectacles and aberred my vision to the liking of the ninety per cent of potential bookbuyers. But I was so prodigiously self-satisfied with my superiority, so flattered by my abnormal normality, that the resource of hypocrisy never occurred to me. Better see rightly on a pound a week than squint on a million."

This extract from the Preface to *Plays Unpleasant,* which by accident I chanced upon when searching for a particular passage, not only epitomises for me both what my grandfather and Shaw, with many others, have suffered because they have seen clearly, but also reminds me of a very happy afternoon spent with Shaw at Ayot St. Lawrence, at which he warned me of the unpopularity and the penury which would face me if I were to persist in the tradition of my grandfather in seeing clearly about the legacy of inefficiency in the communication of the English language by print and hand-writing which the Romans have, with no evil intentions, foisted upon us. At that meeting he recalled my grandfather's fate, described his own, and discussed the future of his own famous Will, which was to be literally his dying effort to persuade others to see this long-standing problem clearly.

To him, to my grandfather, as to me and to anyone who cares to study the subject, it is axiomatic that there should not be the disparity in speed and convenience which still persists between spoken and written communication (see p. 189 for the wording of my grandfather's brilliant exposition of the nature of the problem); that any alphabetic system which continues an alphabetic (and lack of alphabetic) system which was evolved over many hundreds of years in the era before Christ, could certainly not hope to avoid being slow and wearisome, if it had been designed to commemorate enduringly the names, deeds and glories of famous men—Roman soldiers and Emperors; and finally, that it would be inevitably slow, tedious, laborious and wearisome seeing that it had consequently been evolved for execution by chisel and hammer and stone, which was possibly the slowest of all possible forms of written communication, and had not been designed for the modern newspaper press whose speed of communication is that of millions of words a second. To Shaw, to my grandfather, and to anyone who studies it with "normal sight," it has seemed that it ought to be possible, granted the freedom from the fetters of the past and the virgin whiteness of the carte blanche which every real designer demands, to evolve a new and better system of written communication which would be more rapidly written, more easily read and no less beautiful than that which had been thus inherited from the needs of prehistoric times.

It was also axiomatic—to those who thus saw clearly—that there was no subject more fundamental to human progress and thus important, than to ensure that man, that unique animal in his powers of verbal communication, should enjoy in the printed and written language the benefit of modern tools for that purpose.

Just as man is also unique in the delicacy of his vocal organs and in the discriminations which his speech may achieve and his ear appreciate, and is able to communicate by word of mouth efficiently and quickly, so too is he capable of maintaining manual discriminations and of appreciating them visually, and thus to communicate by the printed word. It followed, moreover, from this, that it must be wrong that in the other half of the most important of human attributes, the medium of written words, we should consent to continue forever in a fossilisation of tools, designed for another purpose, appropriate to another language, and virtually unchanged for two millennia:—save for the addition of U and W and the abandonment, in the one regression of the so-called Renaissance, of two characters which had been appropriately designed and used by the Anglo-Saxons for their (and our) non-romanic language.

That passage from Shaw's Preface reminded me, therefore, of a brilliant summer afternoon, and of the drive on 5th August 1947 in the company of Professor Daniel Jones to Ayot St. Lawrence, and the house of Bernard Shaw: of Shaw's invitation, of the post-card telling me how to find the house and of the excitement of our opportunity to meet the great man.

Daniel Jones, as well as being the greatest phonetician and philologist of his time in the English-speaking world, was Chairman of the Simplified Spelling Society, of which I was Treasurer. We had worked long together under the presidency of Sir Gilbert Murray, another world-famous scholar, to perfect an alternative spelling (i.e. alphabetic system)—but one using the familiar roman characters, 23 of them, and 17 digraphs made up of combinations of those characters, viz.:

th dh ch sh zh ng

ae ee ie oe ue aa au oo uu ou oi

and we were hopeful that we would be able to persuade the great G.B.S. to leave his money to our Society, and to prove to him that, in doing so, he would open up the only practical avenue for the achievement of what he desired. We hoped that the S.S.S. would thus be accepted by him as the "chosen instrument" which his printed circular of 1944 (see p. 79) was inviting to take up his money.

The iron gate of Shaw's Corner was open, and we were made by the great man to sense that we were most welcome and important visitors. If we could not see clearly (as we ought to be able to see) we could see clearly at least in part. Even if our failure to see that all efforts at improvement in written communication based on acceptance of the roman alphabet must be foredoomed to failure, at least there was hope: after all, the fact that we saw through a glass darkly showed that he might be able to make us see clearly.

The tea was beautifully served by a parlour maid. The quality of the service and of the food was that of Buckingham Palace on all occasions, and that of the middle class villa on occasions of great importance. His attentiveness to our needs and the charm of his manner have been a memory ever since.

So too was the devastating argument and his determined obstinacy! His eyes and beard, his knickerbocker suit, his refusal to join us even in a cup of tea, and his whole presence made defeat, and certainty that there never would be even hope of success, a stimulating and indeed exciting experience.

It must have been the case that those who visited Shaw for a purpose—one might say to ride on the tiger—came away eaten up by the strength of his argument, but with at any rate a replica of that charming smile which had been on the face of the tiger.

I certainly came away elated in my defeat, smiling happily in the knowledge that we were both right—and that I would forever after be so much stronger in the greater clarity which I had gained, and above all, in seeing clearly how two concepts, hitherto apparently conflicting, were indeed complementary—that our Society's ideas for improving romanic alphabeticism remained even sounder than ever, having withstood his devastating dissection. It was obvious that while he remained adamant on the soundness of his own approach, he had been in that limited respect won over, having turned contemptuous dismissal (however politely phrased) into a mutual respect. We made it obvious that, for our part we, too, were adamant and we, too, in a correction of our misconceptions, listened with excitement to his even grander design, and accepted the soundness of his reasoning.

But from that moment my own approach to the objects of our Society was reoriented. My desire to improve our alphabeticism, using the roman alphabet, was shifted from an intended benefit to the adult literate for continuing use, to a benefit intended rather for the young native child (or older foreigner), beginning to learn to read (or to read and speak); my concept of Shaw's non-romanic alphabeticism shifted from a scatter-brained impracticability to one of a brilliant adventure to supplement our romanic handicapped alphabeticism with a non-romanic one, wisely planned by an untrammelled designer to be at least as practical as had been the planning and design of the arabic numerals which had similarly supplemented the roman ones.

He made many predictions that afternoon. He has been proved right in all of them which have arisen as yet.

He predicted that his Will would be opposed. Indeed it was.

(The opposition started even at the very side of his death-bed, where attempts were made to persuade him to revoke it.) He told us not to worry about such opposition, for he hoped his Will would be opposed—because it would give to the cause we had at heart (in both approaches) the finest advertisement that could ever be hoped for. He has been proved most certainly right. He foretold that if we were to support his Will, it would prevail, but that if we did not it would fail. He assured us that he had taken the very best legal advice and that his proposal for creating an alphabet, printing some of his plays and presenting them to public libraries was a once-for-all finite disposition which would in the end be upheld. He was right again, but little did he suppose how strong would be the forces of opposition, and how close his Will came to total failure—even with my support. He told us that there would be no argument about the alphabet as such, that Englishmen regarded Wills as sacrosanct, and that they would no more question the decisions of his executor as to the shape, name and value of any new character than they would question any of the names given to a child at its christening or to a ship at its ceremonial launching.

However, this is an introduction to a book, not a book in itself. I must not allow memories of a brilliant afternoon stand any longer between you and the book you intend to read.

It is interesting and illuminating. Dr. Tauber has the facts precisely organised and the presentation of them most skillfully arranged.

He himself sees clearly, and has that great gift of helping others to be, in that respect, as Shaw would have it—highly fortunate persons, optically.

CONTENTS

Each selection or group of selections is preceded by an introductory note.

ILLUSTRATIONS

INTRODUCTION

by
Dr. Abraham Tauber

George Bernard Shaw, probably the best known writer of modern times, was so popular that he is known and recognized by his initials alone—GBS.

The basis for Shaw's global fame is, of course, his reputation as an intellect and a dramatist. But very many people know GBS because of his activities and writings on the subject of language—the theme of this book—as well as for the literary prowess that brought him the Nobel Prize in 1925.

Shaw is frequently associated with his innovation of the story of a "fish"—spelled "ghoti"—the "gh" of lau*gh*, the "o" of w*o*men, and the "ti" of na*ti*on—the transliteration "ghoti" representing the sounds of the word "fish," as well as the irrational and inconsistent nature of English spelling. GBS carried on a crusade for Alphabet and Spelling Reform that attracted international attention—culminating in the publicity and controversy over his Will, and the publication of the *Shaw Alphabet Edition of Androcles and the Lion.*

Bernard Shaw's writings—including plays, essays, letters and novels—reflected an early interest in the broad field of language. He dealt with spelling and alphabet reform; better speech and communication; phonetics, dialects and accents; international language and punctuation! *Pygmalion,* Shaw's play on which the musical *My Fair Lady* is based, is perhaps the best known example of his writings on these subjects. But Shaw pursued his catholic interest in these matters in a constant stream, spanning almost seventy-five years of creative production.

GBS' work in language evidenced some of the typical Shavian characteristics. His writings combined propaganda with art; he was didactic and dogmatic. He served as a gadfly and iconoclast. He believed that the enonomic motivation would prove the strongest in gaining adherents and supporters for his point of view.

On the other hand, Shaw's contentions and proposals were revolutionary in this realm, not Fabian or gradualist. He was modest and respectful of scholarship. Ironically enough, he avoided any group association—with the Simplified Spelling Society of Great Britain, for example—that might have realistically advanced his cause. The one area for which he expressed little concern—helping children to learn to read—is the one in which his work is bearing the most fruit.

Shaw's work in the field of language is worthy of serious consideration by students, scholars and the general public, especially during this time when better international communications could play such a major role in our lives. For example, the possibility of choice of an auxiliary or international tongue is an issue raised persistently by Professor Mario A. Pei of Columbia University, most recently through the Association for a World Language. If the choice of international language is to be English, as urged by Sir David Eccles, Minister of Education for Great Britain, and by many others including some from non-English speaking cultural backgrounds, then Shaw's ideas are particularly relevant.

The matters with which Shaw concerned himself are quite significant when applied to the newest developments in teaching children to read. Already, considerable experimentation is being carried on in Great Britain and the United States in the use of the Initial Teaching Medium—Augmented Roman Alphabet, devised by Sir James Pitman, and cognate with many ideas on which Shaw expressed himself.

Nevertheless, sparse attention has been paid to Shaw's ideas in these areas by the scholars, language historians and anthologists. Surprisingly little is reported about Shaw's contributions to these fields in modern studies of language. For example,

Shaw's work suffers undeserved neglect by omission from several recent anthologies of writings on language (cf. N. C. Stageberg's *Introductory Readings on Language*, Holt, Rinehart and Winston, Inc., New York, 1962; C. Laird and R. M. Gorrell's *English as Language: Backgrounds, Development, Usage*, Harcourt and World, Inc., New York, 1961; W. Gibson's *The Limits of Language*, Hill and Wang, New York, 1962) and from proper mention in the 1962 revised edition of Stuart Robinson's *The Development of Modern English*, Prentice-Hall, Inc., Englewood Cliffs, N. J.

The need for a collection of Shaw's writings in this field is apparent. At a time when linguistics, semantics and communications are by-words in liberal education, Shaw's work deserves to be re-examined and kept in mind to provide stimulation and possible guidance.

Jacques Barzun, calling Shaw "the most astonishing mind in two centuries," bestowed on him the accolade of "Western Man," designating him "the greatest master of English prose since Swift." Brooks Atkinson has acclaimed Shaw for his "concern for the welfare of mankind," because "he worked for a better world for everybody." John Gassner appraised Shaw as one of our greatest playwright-propagandists, who brought wit and poetry to the play of ideas. These estimates reflect the judgments of legions of admirers of the Shavian genius.

But Shaw's broad reputation was based also on this other facet of his versatile talents and interests—his writings and activities in the field of Language, the subject of this anthology. That aspect of his work made him known to people all over the world, helping to focus the spotlight on everything else that Shaw did.

Shaw's interest in language spanned his life-period of active writing from 1876 to 1950. Protean in the literary form it took, his preoccupation became more intense with advancing years.

Whence this interest of Shaw in language qua language? GBS was from his earliest days an amateur philologist, as reflected in his own writings and in this observation from Archibald Henderson's biography, *George Bernard Shaw* (1911):

> Together Lecky and Shaw studied and discussed phonetics, and while Shaw's knowledge of the subject was by no means exhaustive, his interest in it has since served as a permanent protection against such superficial catch-penny stuff as the reformed spellings that are invented every six months by faddists. Shaw's individual mode of punctuation, his use of spaced letters in place of italics, his almost total rejection, on Biblical authority, which he accepted for once, of quotation marks, and those numerous original rules of punctuation and phonetics which he has from time to time formulated in magazine and daily press, find their raison d'être in Shaw's early association with Lecky and subsequent acquaintance, through L's instrumentality, with the late Alexander Ellis and Henry Sweet of Oxford.

Born in 1856 in Ireland, GBS came to London in 1876. Evidences of Shaw's interest in the problems and techniques of the language vehicle appeared in his earliest writings, such as the novel, *Immaturity*, published in 1879. There, as in later novels and plays, GBS tried to record the dialect of a character—in this case, one who employed Shaw's own vernacular, Irish-English. GBS continued the same practice with the Scotch dialect of Rankin and the American pronunciation of Kearney, in *Captain Brassbound's Conversion*, and of Hector Malone, in *Man and Superman*, 1903.

Shaw's interest in cockney speech went back to his earliest days in London. In *Love Among The Artists* (1881), Shaw, fresh from Ireland, has Jack say to Magdalen:

> I taught her to make the best of such vowels as there are left in our spoken language.

The hero, probably a prototype of Shaw himself, disliked "the slovenly habits of colloquial speech."

GBS distinguished the cockney dialect he recorded from the

earlier Dickens' variety. His attempted transliterated spellings of the dialect, as found in the speech of Drinkwater (*Captain Brassbound's Conversion*), of Burgess (*Candida*, 1894), of Bill Walker (*Major Barbara*, 1905), and of Liza Doolittle (*Pygmalion*, 1912), were based both on his own observations and on cues taken from scholars whose work he had studied.

Joseph Saxe, a student of cockney dialect, used GBS' writings as the basis for *Bernard Shaw's Phonetics: A Comparative Study of Cockney Sound-Changes*, George Allen and Unwin, Ltd., London, 1936. Though by no means agreeing with all of Shaw's observations about dialect, Saxe found them generally authentic, reliable and uniformly worthy of scholarly consideration.

In this bit of dialogue from *Pygmalion*, Shaw told something of what he learned from Henry Sweet, phonetician, here depicted as Professor Henry Higgins: (See p. 39)

> PICKERING . . . It's a fearful strain. I rather fancied myself because I can pronounce twenty-four distinct vowel sounds; but your hundred and thirty beat me. I can't hear a bit of difference between most of them.
>
> HIGGINS . . . Oh, that comes with practice. You hear no difference at first; but you keep on listening, and presently you find that they are all as different as A from B.

In a talk on "The Problems of English," reported in *The Times* of London for June 17, 1921, Shaw stated that "the last census showed that dialects numbered 42,767,500." GBS had, by that time, become impressed with the variety and individuality of speech, a subject on which he expatiated in the script for the recordings he made for Linguaphone Institute in 1928, reproduced in this book. (See p. 54)

Shaw did not hesitate to spar with the professionals, or anyone who cared to exchange ideas with him. (See p. 9) While GBS boasted of his intimate knowledge of "vowels and consonants as a phonetic expert" in his *Dramatic Essays,* Shaw readily admitted, in *The Morning Leader* of August 22, 1901:

> I am no expert phonetician; but I have heard a great deal of Cockney eloquence from speakers of all classes during the past quarter century; and I have listened to it not only as a politician listens, but as a playwright and a critic, both musical and dramatic, listens. Hence my "amusing tone of authority" on the subject.

Shaw acknowledged his debt to the scholars, as will be seen in the "Preface to *Pygmalion*" (p. 39), in "Notes to *Captain Brassbound's Conversion*" (p. 1), and in sundry letters and essays.

Shaw's authority was challenged by a correspondent in *The Morning Leader* of August 19, 1901:

> I can only suppose that Mr. Shaw is a provincial gentleman who has never been in London. If he should ever pay us a visit, he will find that in no part of the metropolis is the syllable 'ell' pronounced 'yoll.' Let him try the effect of telling a Cockney to go to yoll. It will not be taken as an insult; it will simply be unintelligible.

Shaw replied as follows (p. 20):

> I am far too polite a man to tell any Cockney . . . to go to hell. But every bus conductor in London would understand me perfectly if I told him to let me down at the Queen's Yollm . . . He writes the sound he utters as ell, and is naturally incredulous when I write it yoll. It is precisely because I am "a provincial gentleman" . . . that I am conscious of the aberrations of Cockney pronunciation. A Cockney is unconscious of Cockney pronunciation. . . . (*The Morning Leader*, August 22, 1901)

Dr. Bernard Saxe, quoting the philologist, Otto Jesperson, supports GBS' expert qualifications but suggests that GBS' respelling technique may be a source of misunderstanding, accompanied by some tendency on Shaw's part to exaggerate for purposes of making a point.

Shaw's writings embodying his interest in language continued throughout his career to the last days of his life. The fact that his Will (p. 163) left the income of the residue of his estate to carry out a program of alphabet reform is evidence of his seriousness of purpose in this matter.

Of course, critics of Shaw's ideas and work were numerous and vocal. In the *Morning Leader* of August 27, 1901, one wrote on "G.B.S.'s Phonetics" as follows

> . . . I love the language and revel in its intricacies. In my heart of hearts I despise the man who displaces the *e* and *i* in such words as "receive" and "believe," or who writes dispatch for despatch. Bad spelling, split infinitives, and very glaring faults in grammar, gall and irritate me . . . No, let the language alone and, above all, for pity's sake, don't Americanize it. Don't eliminate precious letters for the sake of extra speed on a typewriter. Don't spell "programme"—"program" or "labour"—"labor." Words have histories and origins; etymology is still studied by some. The plea of the "fonetik" fiend is that his system will help towards a universal pronunciation. Don't believe him, it will not. It is visual atrocity and not to be tolerated by those who have learnt to love the language in its present artistic form.

Shaw did not apply his rhetorical recommendations to his own writings, consistently. Nevertheless, one will notice the general absence of apostrophes, the adoption of spelling "Americanizations" such as "labor" and "program," and the minimum use of commas. (p. 25)

In letters sent to Sir James Pitman, GBS stated his position on a number of language matters. On September 16, 1941, Shaw wrote:

> Dear Mr. Pitman,
>
> If you take up this spelling business it may get a move on after lying fallow for a generation, as you are evidently the grandson of your grandfather, and a chip off the old block.

(The grandfather referred to was Sir Isaac Pitman, spelling reformer and deviser of shorthand.)

In the same letter, Shaw urged "the inevitability of gradualness" in Spelling Reform, or more accurately, Alphabet Reform. He specified a plan—to design an alphabet of 42 letters, publish a manual and a propagandist journal, and transliterate some modern books—like Shaw, "not the Bible or Shakespear," into the New British Writing. These ideas were the same ones he had set forth in 1906 and that were the essence of the plan in his Will, in 1950.

Ironically, in the same letter, Shaw disclaimed any recognition of the name of Godfrey Dewey, whom Pitman commended to him as an American colleague whose ideas were worth considering, in an effort to impress Shaw with the importance of an organized effort, coordinated in America and Britain.

On July 3, 1943, Shaw wrote to Pitman that a certain correspondent with original ideas in the field of language reform "should have studied Sweet and not bothered about the others. He quarreled with everybody; but he was a phonetic genius." This reference to Sweet had been elaborated in the "Preface to *Pygmalion*." On July 20, 1943, Shaw described "the next step, which is to establish a sufficient British alphabet and demonstrate its enormous *saving in labor* no matter at which speed it is written, printed, typed, or acquired by children."

That was the essence of his belief—as he said in the same letter—to "stick to phonetics and economics." GBS wrote in May 17,

1950, in the twilight of his life, that his notion of his contribution to the "phonetic question" was his insistence on the immense saving of labor that could be effected by the general use of a 40 letter alphabet.

Despite his insistence on revolutionary changes, perhaps utopian and quixotic, Shaw always dealt in his writings with such practical language problems as how to speak well and be both intelligible and impressive.

This anthology is a collection of items from a special part of Shaw's versatile repertory. They all deal with how English is and should be spoken, and how to reform its writing and printing to make it easier for people to speak and write it well, and how more efficiently to learn to read and use the language with economy of labor.

There is great public interest in these subjects. What parent has not evinced concern that his child read better and faster, and spell in a reasonable facsimile of the conventional orthography of the language? Should not President Theodore Roosevelt's bout with Congress over spelling reform be taken from the dusty shelves of the archives of history? Even if the debates in Commons over Spelling Reform have been dimmed in memory, the dispute over Shaw's Will lingers on—spurred by the publication of *Androcles and the Lion* in the Shaw Alphabet Edition.

This anthology, which covers fifty years of writing, is offered in chronological arrangement, except for one item grouped by relevance to the subject (p. 174). All the pieces are by Shaw, except for the Commons' Debate (p. 137), the judicial decision on his Will (p. 169), and the four pieces by Sir James Pitman that conclude the volume.

Some may prefer to read by selected themes or pieces, in which event the Table of Contents or Index can serve as a guide. The Shaw materials on language, though not all he wrote, are representative and comprehensive, include the outstandingly important ones, and cover the gamut of Shaw's interests. The notes offer background that should give historical perspective and depth to a true understanding of Shaw's ideas.

The editor would like to express special appreciation to Sir James Pitman, and Professor Dan H. Laurence of New York University, for invaluable aid; to Philosophical Library, the publishers, for cordial cooperation; and to his wife, Rhea, for long and arduous hours of editorial assistance and sympathetic support.

Abraham Tauber, 1963
Bermuda

ACKNOWLEDGMENTS

The Editor wishes to express his thanks to:

Sir James Pitman, for contributing the Foreword and other materials;

Prof. Dan H. Laurence of New York University, for providing access to materials from his extensive files on Shaw;

Dr. Reto Rossetti of Bristol University, for making available his file of original letters from Shaw;

The Society of Authors of London, for license to reprint Shaw materials;

H.M. Stationery Office, London, the Incorporated Council of Law Reporting for England and Wales, the British Esperanto Association, Penguin Books, Ltd., Philosophical Library, the Linguaphone Institute, *The Atlantic Monthly, The Author, The Listener, The Morning Leader, The Quarterly Journal of Speech, The Shavian,* and *The Times* of London, for permission to reprint materials described in the text; The National Gallery of Ireland, for the photograph of Paul Troubetskoy's statue of Shaw.

George Bernard Shaw

ON LANGUAGE

"ENGLISH AND AMERICAN DIALECTS"
from
"NOTES TO *CAPTAIN BRASSBOUND'S CONVERSION*"
(August, 1900)

A modern writer onomatopoeically described President Kennedy as a "public speakah," who appealed to "the American eeah in the lahst yeeah." This method of depicting dialect, speech pattern or pronunciation by respelling words was used by Mark Twain, Finley Peter Dunne, Artemus Ward and Josh Billings. An attempt to read aloud from such writings in the way the author intended is a challenging exercise in phonetics.

George Bernard Shaw used the same respelling technique to delineate how dialogue was to be spoken in his plays. In *Captain Brassbound's Conversion,* for example, Shaw's transliterated orthography was intended to indicate cockney speech and Scotch burr. The unfamiliar appearance of the words in the text of the play succeeded both in baffling the actor and confusing the reader.

First, Shaw described the unmistakable flavor and idiosyncrasies of class origin in the speech of the Cockney. Then, Shaw, the playwright, deplored the inadequacies of respelling for his purposes. He professed futility "without the aid of a phonetic alphabet." Students of phonetics and dialects find it extremely difficult to ascertain precisely what Shaw meant in the opening passages of the introductory note to Act I of *Captain Brassbound's Conversion,* in which GBS described the speech of the London Cockney character, Felix Drinkwater.

His utterance, affectedly pumped and hearty, and naturally vulgar and nasal, is ready and fluent: nature, a Board School education, and some kerbstone practice having made him a bit of an orator. His dialect, apart from its base nasal delivery, is not unlike that of smart London society in its tendency to replace diphthongs by vowels (sometimes rather prettily) and to shuffle all the traditional vowel pronunciations. He pronounces ow as ah, and i as aw, using the ordinary ow for o, i for ā, ă for ŭ, and ĕ for ă, with this reservation, that when any vowel is followed by an r, he signifies its presence, not by pronouncing the r, which he never does under these circumstances, but by prolonging and modifying the vowel, sometimes even to the extreme degree of pronouncing it properly. As to his yol for l (a compendious delivery of the provincial eh-al), and other metropolitan refinements, amazing to all but cockneys, they cannot be indicated, save in the above imperfect manner, without the aid of a phonetic alphabet.

Throughout the play, Shaw continued to use respelling to suggest dialectal flavor, despite his protestations of the technical shortcomings of this method. We have reproduced below from Act I of *Captain Brassbound's Conversion* the first exchange between the Cockney character, Drinkwater, and Mr. Rankin, the Scotch missionary, to illustrate how the author attempted to denote the two dialects.

DRINKWATER. Awtenoon, Mr. Renkin. Yr honor's eolth.

RANKIN. Good afternoon, Mr. Drinkwotter.

DRINKWATER. Youre not best pleased to be hinterrapted in yr bit o gawdnin baw the lawk o me, gavner.

RANKIN. A missionary knows nothing of leks of that soart, or of disleks either, Mr. Drinkwotter. What can I do for ye?

Shaw discussed pronunciation and dialects in English in an epilogue, "Notes to *Captain Brassbound's Conversion.*" That essay contains some cogent comments:

> "The fact that English is spelt conventionally and not phonetically makes the art of recording speech almost impossible . . . I must, however, most vehemently disclaim any intention of suggesting that English pronunciation is authoritative and correct . . . Besides, there is no standard English pronunciation any more than there is an American one . . . nothing annoys a native speaker of English more than a faithful setting down in phonetic spelling of the sounds he utters."

Shaw disdained dogmatizing on standards or setting his own speech as a universal model; this scholarly modesty was to continue throughout his life:

> "My own tongue is neither American English nor English English, but Irish English; so I am as nearly impartial in the matter as it is in human nature to be."

Shaw displayed a thorough understanding of phonetics and exceptionally keen insights and observations for a non-professional. He expatiated on the disparate nature of dialects, and the necessity for up-dating of cockney from the "Dickens dialect." As a versatile amateur, his virtuosity in the field antedated America's H. L. Mencken by many decades.

NOTES TO
CAPTAIN BRASSBOUND'S CONVERSION
(August, 1900)

"English and American Dialects"

The fact that English is spelt conventionally and not phonetically makes the art of recording speech almost impossible. What is more, it places the modern dramatist, who writes for America as well as England, in a most trying position. Take for example my American captain and my English lady. I have spelt the word conduce, as uttered by the American captain, as cawndooce, to suggest (very roughly) the American pronunciation to English readers. Then why not spell the same word, when uttered by Lady Cicely, as kerndewce, to suggest the English pronunciation to American readers? To this I have absolutely no defence: I can only plead that an author who lives in England necessarily loses his consciousness of the peculiarities of English speech, and sharpens his consciousness of the points in which American speech differs from it; so that it is more convenient to leave English peculiarities to be recorded by American authors. I must, however, most vehemently disclaim any intention of suggesting that English pronunciation is authoritative and correct. My own tongue is neither American English nor English English, but Irish English; so I am as nearly impartial in the matter as it is in human nature to be. Besides, there is no standard English pronunciation any more than there is an American one: in England every county has its catchwords, just as no doubt every State in the Union has. I cannot believe that the pioneer American, for example, can spare time to learn that last refinement of modern speech, the exquisite diphthong, a farfetched combination of the French eu and the English e, with which a New Yorker pronounces such words as world, bird, &c. I have spent months without success in trying to achieve glibness with it.

To Felix Drinkwater also I owe some apology for implying that all his vowel pronunciations are unfashionable. They are very far from being so. As far as my social experience goes (and I have kept very mixed company) there is no class in English society in which a good deal of Drinkwater pronunciation does not pass unchallenged save by the expert phonetician. This is no mere rash and ignorant jibe of my own at the expense of my English neighbors. Academic authority in the matter of English speech is represented at present by Mr. Henry Sweet, of the University of Oxford, whose *Elementarbuch des gesprochenen Englisch,* translated into his native language for the use of British islanders as a Primer of Spoken English, is the most accessible standard work on the subject. In such words as plum, come, humbug, up, gun, etc., Mr. Sweet's evidence is conclusive. Ladies and gentlemen in Southern England pronounce them as plam, kam, hambag, ap, gan, etc., exactly as Felix Drinkwater does. I could not claim Mr. Sweet's authority if I dared to whisper that such coster English as the rather pretty dahn tahn for down town, or the decidedly ugly cowcow for cocoa is current in very polite circles. The entire nation, costers and all, would undoubtedly repudiate any such pronunciation as vulgar. All the same, if I were to attempt to represent current "smart" cockney speech as I have attempted to represent Drinkwater's, without the niceties of Mr. Sweet's Romic alphabets, I am afraid I should often have to write dahn tahn and cowcow as being at least nearer to the actual sound than down town and cocoa. And this would give such offence that I should have to leave the country; for nothing annoys a native speaker of English more than a faithful setting down in phonetic spelling of the sounds he utters. He imagines that a departure from conventional spelling indicates a departure from the correct standard English of good society. Alas! this correct standard English of good society is unknown to phoneticians. It is only one of the many figments that bewilder our poor snobbish brains. No such thing exists; but what does that matter to people trained from infancy to make a point of honor of belief in abstractions and incredibilities? And so I am compelled to hide Lady Cicely's speech under the veil of conventional orthography.

I need not shield Drinkwater, because he will never read my book. So I have taken the liberty of making a special example of him, as far as that can be done without a phonetic alphabet, for the benefit of the mass of readers outside London who still form their notions of cockney dialect on Sam Weller. When I came to London in 1876, the Sam Weller dialect had passed away so completely that I should have given it up as a literary fiction if I had not discovered it surviving in a Middlesex village, and heard of it from an Essex one. Some time in the eighties the late Andrew Tuer called attention in the Pall Mall Gazette to several peculiarities of modern cockney, and to the obsolescence of the Dickens dialect that was still being copied from book to book by authors who never dreamt of using their ears, much less of training them to listen. Then came Mr. Anstey's cockney dialogues in Punch, a great advance, and Mr. Chevalier's coster songs and patter. The Tompkins verses contributed by Mr. Barry Pain to the London Daily Chronicle also did something to bring the literary convention for cockney English up to date. But Tompkins sometimes perpetuated horrible solecisms. He would pronounce face as fice, accurately enough; but he would rhyme it quite impossibly to nice, which Tompkins would have pronounced as nawce: for example Mawl Enn Rowd for Mile End Road. This aw for i, which I have made Drinkwater use, is the latest stage of the old diphthongal oi, which Mr. Chevalier still uses. Irish, Scotch, and north country readers must remember that Drinkwater's rs are absolutely unpronounced when they follow a vowel, though they modify the vowel very considerably. Thus, though luggage is pronounced by him as laggige, turn is not pronounced as tarn, but as teun with the eu sounded as in French. The London r seems thoroughly understood in America, with the result, however, that the use of the r by Artemus Ward and other American dialect writers causes Irish people to misread them grotesquely. I once saw the pronunciation of *malheureux* represented in a cockney handbook by mal-err-err: not at all a bad makeshift to instruct a Londoner, but out of the question elsewhere in the British Isles. In America, representations of English speech dwell too derisively on the dropped or interpolated h. American writers have apparently not noticed the fact that the south English h is not the same as the never-dropped Irish and American h, and that to ridicule an Englishman for dropping it is as absurd as to ridicule the whole French and Italian nation for doing the same. The American h, helped out by a general agreement to pronounce wh as hw, is tempestuously audible, and cannot be dropped without being immediately missed. The London h is so comparatively quiet at all times, and so completely inaudible in wh, that it probably fell out of use simply by escaping the ears of children learning to speak. However that may be, it is kept alive only by the literate classes who are reminded constantly of its existence by seeing it on paper. Roughly speaking, I should say that in England he who bothers about his hs is a fool, and he who ridicules a dropped h a snob. As to the interpolated h, my experience as a London vestryman has convinced me that it is often effective as a means of emphasis, and that the London language would be poorer without it. The objection to it is no more respectable than the objection of a street boy to a black man or to a lady in knickerbockers.

I have made only the most perfunctory attempt to represent the dialect of the missionary. There is no literary notation for the grave music of good Scotch.

BLACKDOWN,
August 1900.

"SPELLING REFORM v. PHONETIC SPELLING A PLEA FOR SPEECH NATIONALISATION"

The Morning Leader (London) (August 16, 1901)

"Spelling Reform v. Phonetic Spelling, A Plea for Speech Nationalisation" is a polemical rejoinder to the moderate views of two spelling reformers: Columbia University Professor Brander Matthews, who had written "The Simplification of English Spelling" for *Century Magazine,* of August 1901; and GBS' friend, William Archer, responsible for "Spelling Reform or Phonetic Spelling" in *The Morning Leader* of August 10, 1901.

Matthews and Archer had dismissed as "impracticable" the phonetic ideal in spelling reform, *i.e.,* completely revised orthography, favoring a gradual revision as more likely to conserve the stabilizing influence of conventional spelling for clear pronunciation and to correct the prevalent slovenliness of speech. Archer deplored "how far the ordinary pronunciation even of educated men slurs the ideal sonorities of the language." Matthews contended that orthography in the United States "is in a healthier state than it is in Great Britain, where there is a closer approximation to a deadening uniformity."

GBS accepted the importance of spelling as a guide to pronunciation. He conceded the lessened tendency to substitute the w for v sound in cockney speech: "The moment the masses learnt to read, they stopped saying 'werry' for 'very,' and 'inwaluable' for 'invaluable.' Just so far as our spelling was phonetic, it helped and corrected them."

Shaw noted that "the influence of the printed word over pronunciation can hardly be exaggerated." But, extending the principle to its logical conclusion, he interpreted this fact as a further advantage of completely phonetic spelling: "The flagrant corruptions of the sounds are directly due to the unphonetic spelling of our established orthography, and nothing but a thorough reform will avail." His arguments can be summed up in the statement: "You must either let our spelling alone or else reform it phonetically." This was and is the position of the British Simplified Spelling Society, although they would prefer the word *phonemically* to describe their "World English Spelling." Such a "*phonemic* reform" Shaw later rejected for his Will. (See "Foreword," pages VII to XII.) Shaw distinguished carefully between "spelling reform" and "phonetic spelling," and strongly advocated the latter, as Archibald Henderson recorded in his authorized biography of 1911, *George Bernard Shaw.*

In his own writing, Shaw used orthodox spellings for the most part. His deviations and variants from the British standard were sporadic vagaries—*labor, alfabetic, youre,* etc. He believed categorically that spelling modifications short of the whole effort were negligible in effect (which he spelled *negligeable* in *Cashel Byron's Profession*).

Subsequently, Shaw went beyond the advocacy of phonetic spelling to a proposal for adoption of a completely new alphabet for the English language, as the best and only solution to the spelling dilemma.

In this letter sent to the *Morning Leader*, Shaw used the schwa (ə) to illustrate the phonetic principle. Even more significant is his discussion of the importance of a knowledge of phonetics in teaching speech and the improved use of the English language. This idea later materialised, of course, into *Pygmalion* with Prof. Higgins and Eliza Doolittle exemplifying the idea. At this point in his thinking, Shaw thought of the goal of phonetics and spelling reform as good speech, even more important than easing the learning of reading. Later he was to shift his emphasis to the economics of alphabet and spelling reform.

SPELLING REFORM V.

PHONETIC SPELLING.

A PLEA FOR SPEECH NATIONALISATION

By G. Bernard Shaw

(August 16, 1901)

TO THE EDITOR OF "THE MORNING LEADER"

Sir,—I have not read Professor Brander Matthews's article on this subject and I am for the moment out of reach of a bookstall; but the "Study and Stage" essay of my friend Mr. William Archer on the subject provokes me to add a couple of thousand words or so.

Mr. Archer throws over the Columbian snob to whose belated ignorance spelling reform is "hopelessly, unspeakably, sickeningly vulgar." And he throws the established orthography after him. But he insists on the need for a conventional spelling, and declares that it must not be a phonetic spelling. Yet I may take it, I think, that he does not want a Chinese ideography, or a hieroglyphic system. What, then, does he want? At one point in his article he suggests a spelling of the language as it would sound if it were declaimed poetically, and with the obscure vowels pronounced like the letters that are used haphazardly to represent them in our conventional orthography. Thus the obscure vowel in absurd would be pronounced like a in cab, that in enough or peculiar like e in be. But this would be a phonetic spelling just as much as Mr. Sweet's Romic, though it would represent, not the sounds that we utter, but the sounds that

Mr. Archer thinks he hears in his mind's ear when he reads poetry, or, to use his own phrase, "the ideal sonorities of the language."

Further on, Mr. Archer says that what he wants to reform is not conventional spelling, but a number of needless and absurd anomalies of convention. By this I understand him to mean that it is a needless and absurd anomaly to spell telegram telegram and programme programme. So it is; but how would Mr. Archer propose to reform the anomaly? Apparently, not by spelling programme program, because that would be choosing the phonetic principle, which he denounces as "noxious." He would therefore spell telegram telegramme, and so remove the anomaly without phonetic noxiousness. He would spell off "ough" and trite "tright," Lumley "Lolmondeley," and Holborn "Hockburn." Or rather he would do nothing of the sort, but would write another "Study and Stage" article, confessing that Voltaire's are not the only principles that "lead to their logical conclusion." Besides, if so, why push them? I am quite ready to let Mr. Archer off if he will let off Voltaire.

The fact is, you must either let our spelling alone or else reform it phonetically. No sane person now proposes to reform it "etymologically"; and once the etymological aberration is outlived, nothing remains to be spelt except sound. Our alphabet is a phonetic one as far as it goes; and our established spelling is phonetic spelling, partly out of date, and partly corrupted by an ignorant academic attempt to make it etymological. Discard the etymologic blunder, and you cannot predicate either rationality or anomaly for our spelling except in reference to phonetic propriety and consistency. Rule out phonetics, and "programme" remains neither an irrational spelling nor an anomalous one: it is simply a French spelling; and the sole objection to it is that in English it is unphonetic; and leads the people who have never heard it pronounced to say programmy, and the people who have never seen it written to write program, and be humiliated and snubbed by the empty uppish, a class ably represented by the Columbian University bounder quoted by Professor Brander Matthews.

And, now, what harm does our spelling do to literature? Among other things, it so obscures the history of the language as to make even a literary expert like Mr. Archer commit himself in print to the undownliveable statement (if only he really meant it) that the English language has hardly drifted since Shakespear's time because it has been anchored to the rock of a conventional spelling. As a matter of fact, Shakespear's English is a dead language. No living man can speak it or write it. He can imitate it just as Milton and Landor imitated Latin poetry; and people with a literary turn can understand it without difficulty. Mr. Archer has, no doubt, become so accustomed to it that it no longer strikes him as archaic: but let him ask a policeman the way to Hanwell in the best Elizabethan he can muster, and that policeman will probably see that he arrives there. And we need not go back so far as Shakespear. No metropolitan Englishman can now write or speak eighteenth century English, though Irish and Scotch writers still use modified Augustan. Early nineteenth century English is equally obsolete to young men. No journalist under forty could write anything like one of the "Sketches by Boz."

All this Mr. Archer, of course, knows as well as I do. Then what does he mean by saying that the language has not changed? Probably nothing more than that most of the words in Shakespear's vocabulary are still in use, a statement which, applied to so short a period of time as nine or ten generations, is not worth making. Words last a long time; and the highest literary expression changes slowly from one great master to another; but vernacular locutions change very rapidly: for example, the "whoreson knaves" of the sixteenth century become, in the paragraphs of modest police-court reporters, the — —s of the nineteenth. Our conventional spelling has not hindered any of these changes: they would have occurred at the same rate if the English language had been spelt all the time on the Weller principle, "according to the taste and fancy of the speller." All that the conventional spelling has done is to conceal the one change that a phonetic spelling might have checked: namely, the changes in pronunciation, including the waves of debasement that produced the half rural cockney of Sam Weller, and the modern metropolitan cockney of Drinkwater in "Captain Brassbound's Conversion." At all events, here alone was the establishment and maintenance of a standard humanly possible: for the influence of the printed word over pronunciation can hardly be exaggerated. The moment the masses learnt to read, they stopped saying "werry" for "very," and "inwaluable" for "invaluable." Just so far as our spelling was phonetic, it helped and corrected them. But just so far as it was unphonetic, it misled them; and before Mr. Archer is an old man he will be ridiculed as a fogey unless he yields to the overwhelming currency of modern mispronunciations founded on the phonetic suggestions of our half phonetic spelling. If we, the literary men, will not spell as we pronounce, the world will end by pronouncing as we spell. For instance, we spelt obleege oblige, to show that we were French scholars; and now we are forced to say oblige. If Archer were spelt Ariqricher, the familiar name "William Ought-jer" would be unknown in London. Beauchamp's Pills would never be deemed worth a guinea a box. We cannot prevent people from interpreting our spelling phonetically: there is no other way of interpreting it for people whose vocabulary is not literary nor even always printable. What does Mr. Archer himself do when he comes upon the name of a Russian statesman in print? He pronounces it as the spelling suggests, just as his great-great grandfather pronounced the name of Handel. And, like his ancestor, he pronounces it wrongly. But as everybody else in England, except perhaps the diplomatic staff, does the same, his wrong pronunciation becomes the standard one; and an Englishman pronouncing the Russian name properly becomes as insufferable and unintelligible as if he were to talk about Hendel. In vain will Mr. Archer urge his readers to act like logical Scotchmen, and, recognising the fact that our spelling is not perfectly phonetic, refrain from drawing phonetic inferences from it. We cannot draw any other inferences from it: if we want to use the word and are not on speaking terms with anybody who knows how to pronounce it we *must* pronounce it as it is spelt or misspelt, as the case may be. Refuse to teach the Board School legions your pronunciation, and they will force theirs on you by mere force of numbers. And serve you right!

And here I come to the real question which has extracted this long letter from me—the question of the nationalisation of the existing class monopoly of orthodox English speech. The only English schools now worth counting are the schools under the Education Department: the only important universities are the Polytechnics. From them we are turning out hosts of young men about ten times as full of primary and secondary instruction as Mr. Archer was when he graduated at Edinburgh, Mr. Walkley when he graduated at Oxford, or as I am to this day. They are a new race; and Mr. H. G. Wells is probably right in anticipating that they will finally become the dominant force in our social organisation. But they speak, not of the sun and moon, but of the san and mə-oon. (I use the inverted e for that obscure vowel which offends Mr. Archer in "absurd.") Tea and coffee they call tə-ee and corfee. Now san for sun does not matter; for though Gladstone would have scorned it, to-day it has become the received Oxford-West-end pronunciation. But the young man who says mə-oon and tə-ee, or in a political conference calls himself a delegite, or perhaps a dyollagite, will find these solecisms obstructing his way through life more than three or four sentences of imprisonment would obstruct a peer's. Yet, if matters are left as they are, he will undoubtedly triumph in the long run, and force the smart people to say "mə-oon" and "delegite," as he has already forced them to say "dahn tahn" for down town (which is rather pretty), and "ow now" for "oh no" (which is detestable). But he himself does not want to be let alone. He already takes the greatest pains to speak well by the fatal process of imitation, and succeeds mostly only in adding affectation to mispronunciation. Why will not Mr. Archer let him be taught in the only possible way, by instruction in the phonetic alphabet, and by having a standard pronunciation suggested to him on every printed page? Mr. Archer supposes that practical phonetics are impossibly complex and difficult. That is a novice's notion. The subtle differences of which Mr. Archer is thinking do not trouble experts at all: there may be six-and-thirty ways of saying "get" (and "every single one of them is right"), just as there may be six-and-thirty ways of saying "git" (and every single one of them is wrong); but that does not in the slightest degree complicate the simple process of teaching a child to say get instead of git. I put it to friend William, does he seriously suppose that when a Frenchman goes to the Reader of Phonetics at Oxford to be taught to pronounce English, Mr. Sweet has any difficulty in teaching him? He does not even require a special type for his reading lessons: ordinary type can be made to suffice when the vowels are eked out by turning e and c upside down occasionally. In short, the supposed complication does not exist. Mr. Archer may dream of a script that would distinguish between the voice and speech of Miss Ellen Terry and the voice and speech of Mrs. Patrick Campbell; but nobody proposes to go into such subtleties in a board school class-room. What is proposed, and what is perfectly feasible, is a script which shall distinguish between the correctness of speech common to both these ladies, and the quaint slavey lingo of Miss Louie Frecar.

I am convinced that such instruction would be popular. Once, years ago, I was asked to go down to the docks and give a few young dock laborers a lecture on elocution to refine the oratory of the "New Unionism" of that period. They probably expected me to spout Shakespear to them. Instead, I discoursed on their phonetic alphabet. They were sufficiently amused to tell me I ought to be "a quick-change artist"; but they were also keenly interested, because they were quite aware that there was a difference for the worse between their pronunciation and, say, Mr. Archer's; but the nature of that difference—which they earnestly desired to remove—was a mystery to them.

I need not repeat familiar arguments about the waste of teachers' time, and the difficulties thrown in the way of English children learning to read their own language; or the fact that nobody without a *visual* memory for words ever succeeds in spelling conventionally, however highly educated he or she may be; or the barrier placed between England and France by both nations using their printing presses to conceal their language from one another; or the drifting away of colonial and American speech from English for want of a common standard; or the moral mischief of encouraging stupid habits and inventing bad excuses for persisting in them, and so on.

But I do beg Mr. Archer and my contemporaries generally either to let this subject alone or at least take the trouble to acquaint themselves with the latest lights on it. It is shocking to see a paper like "The Morning Leader" beginning the century as the vehicle of the University Conservatisms of the sixties. No doubt the subject is painfully associated in the minds of most middle-aged journalists with early unsuccessful attempts to master the thoroughly bad system of shorthand which was so ably pushed commercially by the late Sir Isaac Pitman, and with the Tonic Sol Fa notation, the Decimal system, the cabbage and rice stage of vegetarianism, and even with Robert Owen's New Moral World, all of which got quaintly mixed up with Spelling Reform in the last century. But now that a Readership of Phonetics has been established at Oxford, and the subject has been worked at throughout Europe by scholars of a very different stamp to Sir Isaac, all that is *vieux jeu.* Spelling Reform may not matter to Mr. Archer, who speaks correctly without knowing anything about phonetics, just as Mr. Walkley wrote grammatically long before I taught him to distinguish prepositions from adverbs; but to the enormous majority of their fellow-townsmen, persistence in our spelling means that worst of handicaps in life, the Board School alphabet of I, Bə-ee, Sə-ee, Də-ee, əee, Af, Jə-ee, Iche, Aw, Ji, Ki, Yoll, Am, An, Ow, Pə-ee, Kə-oo, Awr, Ass, Təee, Yə-oo, Vəee, Dablyəoo, Ax, Waw, Zad.

G. BERNARD SHAW

*PHONETIC SPELLING.**

A REPLY TO SOME CRITICISMS.

By G. Bernard Shaw.

(August 22, 1901)

TO THE EDITOR OF "THE MORNING LEADER"

Sir,—I am far too polite a man to tell any Cockney, as Mr. W. F. Dunton suggests, to go to hell. But every bus conductor in London would understand me perfectly if I told him to let me down at the Queen's Yollm. It is clear from Mr. Dunton's letter that he himself pronounces l as yoll. That is the only possible explanation of his statement that "in no part of the metropolis is the syllable ell pronounced yoll." He writes the sound he utters as ell, and is naturally incredulous when I write it yoll. It is precisely because I am "a provincial gentleman" (in Brixton my native country is considered a province of England) that I am conscious of the aberrations of Cockney pronunciation. A Cockney is unconscious of Cockney pronunciation, just as he is unconscious of the taste of water—because it is always in his mouth. All men, without exception, when first confronted with a phonetic representation of their own speech, vehemently repudiate its accuracy.

* * *

*The matter raged in the letter columns of the *Morning Leader*, with letters impugning Shaw's knowledge of phonetics, his ability to discern a Cockney accent, his status as an expert, and the reliability of his observations and judgments. It reached a climax when a question was raised about specific matters of Cockney accent, and elicited this reply from GBS.

But I appeal to Mr. Dunton, and to Mr. S. K. Ratcliffe, not to confuse the issue by discussing the precision of my necessarily very imperfect attempts to represent Cockney speech. Granted that I am wrong, the question of reforming our spelling remains exactly where it did.

At the same time, I may as well remark that, so far, I am right. Mr. Ratcliffe tells me that i is not pronounced aw in London. But he does not know whether it is or not. If he did, he would not only deny my version but give his own. Mr. Chevalier gives the sound as oi or awy; but that is already a countrified, elderly pronunciation. Nobody in London talks of the Moyle End Road: it is now always the Mawl en Rowd, the tendency to get from diphthongs to pure vowels being as marked in this as in the substitution of ah for ow. I defy Mr. Ratcliffe to suggest any recognisably Cockney pronunciation of i that is not either oi, aw, or one of the stages by which the first has, by dropping its second vowel, changed into the second.

The form "erquittid" for acquitted, given by Mr. Ratcliffe, is simply the received pronunciation. Nobody off the stage says ack-quitted. Now, in writing the part of Drinkwater, from which Mr. Ratcliffe quotes "hacquittid" as an error, I resorted to phonetic spelling only when I wished to indicate that Drinkwater departed from the conventional pronunciation. Mr. Ratcliffe will find, if he tries dialect writing in popular fiction, that this is a necessity of the case. Consequently, instead of writing "herquittid," which would have disguised the word unnecessarily, I took the conventional form "acquitted," and simply put the h to it. Mr. Ratcliffe thinks that I have overdone this added h. I can assure him, with perfect confidence, that he underestimates its prevalence. In oratorical Cockney—which is Drinkwater's specialty—the added h positively rages for the sake of emphasis. The social gulf between Drinkwater and a vestryman is enormous; but the London vestryman, who became extinct only a year ago, was quite familiar with the emphatic added h in debate. And if Mr. Ratcliffe ever enters into correspondence with the class about midway between the vestryman, shopkeeper, and Drinkwater, he will find is and as constantly written his and has.

* * *

I do not deny that "hoonawtid" for united looks grotesque. But I challenge Mr. Ratcliffe to improve on that version. If he says hoonawtid, or, as Mr. Dunton would perhaps prefer it, hoonortid, he will be surprised to hear himself talking exactly like a Cockney. It is because he does not so speak that he finds Cockney grotesque. I am familiar with Mr. Ratcliffe's oratory on the platform, and his speech in private life. He could no more call chance chawnce, or at et, than he could talk Chinese. He pronounces gold goh-oold instead of gahoold. He is anti-Cockney, in fact. But to tell me that my observation has "played me false in a ludicrous degree," because I represented a Lambeth Hooligan as speaking anti-Ratcliffe, is to imply that everyone in London speaks as well as he. I wish everybody did; but that wish can only be achieved through phonetic spelling.

Mr. Ratcliffe may take it from me that the Oxford-

West End ow now for oh no, consists of the same vowels as the coster's. But the coster shuts his nose when he speaks, and so produces a snarl, of which no Oxford man dare be guilty.

In conclusion, let me warn all and sundry that it is quite useless to enter into controversies as to pronunciation merely in a fit of incredulity at the absurd appearance of phonetic spelling. If Mr. Ratcliffe or Mr. Dunton will take the 24 vowels and diphthongs described in, say, Sweet's "Elements of Spoken English," and systematically ascertain how an average costermonger pronounces them, and how he modifies them when certain consonants are ahead of him, then they will be able to handle the subject positively, and perhaps convict me of error. I am no expert phonetician; but I have heard a great deal of Cockney eloquence from speakers of all classes during the past quarter century; and I have listened to it not only as a politician listens, but as a playwright and a critic, both musical and dramatic, listens. Hence my "amusing tone of authority" on the subject.

Mr. Ratcliffe ought to study the subject, because he can exert valuable influence, both as a writer and a speaker, in favor of spelling reform. And Mr. Dunton might well do the same, as his discovery that mat is pronounced met in Cockney shows that he has a good ear, in spite of his insensibility to the remarkable l which I have striven to suggest by yoll. With such an ear, he will, mark my words, end as a spyolling reformer.—Yours, &c.,

G. BERNARD SHAW.

"NOTES ON THE CLARENDON PRESS RULES FOR COMPOSITORS AND READERS"

The Author (April 1, 1902)

Shaw set forth in the British journal for professional writers his notions on many aspects of usage as they apply to the writer, reader and printer. Like Benjamin Franklin, GBS not only wrote on this subject, but was interested as well in spelling reform.

Shaw offered a rationale for the variant forms he used throughout his writing. GBS detailed his unorthodox views toward conventional practices in writing and spelling, expressing preference for "the sensible and reasonable thing" over "the thing that everybody else does."

GBS utilized this opportunity to enunciate some of his phonetic principles, as well. Shaw assailed the "deliberate impoverishment of our insufficient alphabet." He lamented: "That is the worst of unphonetic spelling: in the long run people pronounce words as they are spelt." He observed that "the poverty of the rules *shews* how far we still are from having an accurate speech notation . . . as the desperate phonetics of our dialect novels *show.*" (*Italics mine.* Note the inconsistent spelling of "shews" and "show," not unusual for Shaw—even in the same article—probably to indicate his annoyance with "Johnsonese" orthography.)

Notes on the Clarendon Press Rules for Compositors and Readers

The Author (April 1, 1902)

General Observation.

An author should know his business well enough to be able to settle all these matters by simply writing "follow copy" on his MS. However, as literary talent does not alway include spelling, punctuation, or the faintest sense of beauty in books considered as objects to be looked at as well as read, it is as well that rules should be made for the incapable.

Pages 7, 8. *Spelling.*

As *s* and *z* mark distinct sounds, and the suppression of *z* is a deliberate impoverishment of our insufficient alphabet, the termination *ize* ought to be used in every word that is not common enough to have made the *ise* irresistibly familiar. Advertize, analyze, circumcize, emprize, improvize, mainprize, minimize and paralize, could all be established with much less friction than tantalize, criticize, exorcize, equalize, dogmatize, pulverize, &c., as recommended.

Page 9. *Footnote.*

Dr. Murray's attempt to restore the *e* after *dg* does not really save any ambiguity in the pronunciation. The only cases of g being hard after *d* are Ludgate, Fladgate, etc. A foreigner might, on the analogy of Ludgate, pronounce judgement jud-ge-ment; but no human mouth could pronounce judgment with a hard g.

Spelling generally.

I always use the American termination *or* for *our*. Theater, somber, center, etc., I reject only because they are wantonly anti-phonetic: theatre, sombre, etc., being nearer the sound. Such abominable Frenchifications as programme, cigarette, etc., are quite revolting to me. Telegram, quartet, etc., deprive them of all excuse. I should like also to spell epilogue epilog, because people generally mispronounce it, just as they would mispronounce catalogue if the right sound were not so familiar. That is the worst of unphonetic spelling: in the long run people pronounce words as they are spelt; and so the language gets senselessly altered.

Page 15. *Contractions.*

The apostrophies (*sic*) in ain't, don't, haven't, etc., look so ugly that the most careful printing cannot make a page of colloquial dialogue as handsome as a page of classical dialogue. Besides, shan't should be sha"n't, if the wretched pedantry of indicating the elision is to be carried out. I have written aint, dont, havnt, shant, shouldnt and wont for twenty years with perfect impunity, using the apostrophe only where its omission would suggest another word: for example, hell for he'll. There is not the faintest reason for persisting in the ugly and silly trick of peppering pages with these uncouth bacilli. I also write thats, whats, lets, for the colloquial forms of that is, what is, let us; and I have not yet been prosecuted.

Page 18. *Hyphens.*

I think some of the hyphens given are questionable. Smallpox is right; and small pox is right; but small-pox is, I should say, certainly wrong. A hyphen between an adverb and a verb, or an adjective and a noun, is only defensible when the collocation would be ambiguous without it. The rule given that compound words of more than one accent should be hyphened is, like most rules, a mere brazening-out of a mistake.

Page 21. *Division of English Words.*

The notion that words at the end of a line should not be divided if the division can possibly be avoided leads to a great deal of villainous printing, because the compositor gets it into his head that he may justify recklessly provided he ends the line without breaking a word. I had much rather see even a syllable divided than a line spaced so widely as to make a whitish bar across the black of the letterpress. The compositor should be taught that the evenness of the color of his letterpress is far more important than the philological pedantries of word division. Even from the pedantic point of view there is no sense in recommending impor-tance and respon-dent, and barring exal-tation and imagi-nation. If it is wrong to divide the last syllables of exalt and imagine, it is equally wrong to divide the last syllables of import and respond.

Page 22. Punctuation.

Stops are clearly as much the author's business as words. The rules given here are very properly confined to matters of custom in printing. I wish, however, that the Clarendon Press, or some other leading house, would make a correct rule for the punctuation of quotations between inverted commas. The common practice is to put the points belonging to the sentence in which the quotation occurs inside the inverted commas instead of outside. For example: Was he wise to say "Let us eat and drink; for to-morrow we die?" The correct, but less usual punctuation is: Was he wise to say "Let us eat and drink; for to-morrow we die"?

Page 23. Italics.

This is deplorable. To the good printer the occurrence of two different founts on the same page is at best an unavoidable evil. To the bad one, it is an opportunity of showing off the variety of his stock: he is never happier than when he is setting up a title-page in all the founts he possesses. Not only should titles not be printed in italic; but the customary ugly and unnecessary inverted commas should be abolished. Let me give a specimen. 1. I was reading The Merchant of Venice. 2. I was reading "The Merchant of Venice." 3. I was reading *The Merchant of Venice*. The man who cannot see that No. 1 is the best looking as well as the sufficient and sensible form, should print or write nothing but advertisements of lost dogs or ironmongers' catalogues: literature is not for him to meddle with.

On the whole, and excepting expressly the deplorable heresy about italics, these Clarendon Press rules will serve the turn of the numerous authors who have no ideas of their own on the subject, or who are still in their apprenticeship, or who, as English gentlemen, desire to do, not the sensible and reasonable thing, but the thing that everybody else does. At the same time, the poverty of the rules shews how far we still are from having an accurate speech notation. To the essayist and the scientific writer this may not greatly matter; but to the writer of fiction, especially dramatic fiction, it is a serious drawback, as the desperate phonetics of our dialect novels show. Now the Clarendon Press prints for the essayist and the professor much more than for the fictionist. I therefore suggest that some well-known printer of novels should be asked for a copy of his rules, if he has any. A Scotch printer for preference, as the Scotch intellect likes to know what it is doing.

G. Bernard Shaw

"THE SIMPLIFIED SPELLING PROPOSALS"

Letter to *The Times* of London (September 25, 1906)

Shaw's interest in the phonetics and spelling reform of the English language stemmed from his early contacts with two scholars: Henry Sweet, whom he met through James Lecky in 1879, and Alexander J. Ellis. Both language scholars had been associated in the mid-nineteenth century spelling reform activities of Sir Isaac Pitman, the shorthand inventor. Ellis, Pitman and Sweet became officers of the British Spelling Reform Association when it was founded in 1879.

America has had some distinguished workers for spelling reform. Well known among the early advocates were Benjamin Franklin, Noah Webster and Horace Mann. Later, the National Education Association was the scene of many proposals in this field. In 1906, Melvil Dewey, a founder in 1876 of the Spelling Reform Association, secured philanthropist Andrew Carnegie's support for spelling reform activities. Dewey and Professor Brander Matthews of Columbia University organized a group of renowned philologists and lexicographers into the Simplified Spelling Board.

The Board's plans, publications and activities won President Theodore Roosevelt's approval. On August 27, 1906, President Roosevelt directed the Public Printer to use a list of 300 simplified spellings recommended by the Simplified Spelling Board, e.g., *altho, catalog, center, honor, jail, labor, program, tho, thru,* and *whisky,* in all U.S. Government publications of the Executive Department. This action aroused Congressional criticism and attracted international attention, including expressions of both support and disapproval for the spelling reform activities.

Shaw wrote a letter to *The Times* of London, setting forth his position in the controversy. He agreed with President Roosevelt and the American spelling reformers that English spelling is unphonetic and "pseudo-etymological." Conventional English spelling he contemptuously dubbed "Johnsonese," in derogation of the lexicographic work of Samuel Johnson, whose 1755 *A Dictionary of the English Language* did much to stabilize and fix English spelling in the mold in which we know it. But Shaw visited a plague on both houses—condemning the "shortened" rather than "simplified" spelling of the reformers, itself not "phonetic."

Shaw pointed out that the spelling of English prevented its adoption as "a universal language both for writing and speech." GBS rejected the comparatively mild, gradualistic, "Fabian" remedy of reforming the anachronistic orthography by eliminating superfluous letters and establishing a degree of consistency, the program of the Simplified Spelling Board. He called the reforms "indistinguishable from wrong spelling."

GBS espoused a new English alphabet—with a newly devised symbol for each of the forty-odd sounds. The Shavian prescription for the confused orthographic state, as early as 1906, was radical, requiring the enlargement of the alphabet by the addition of artistically designed symbols.

On September 25, 1906, the following letter from Shaw appeared in *The Times* of London. His views on spelling and alphabet reform remained substantially the same down to the day he expressed them in his Will in 1950.

THE SIMPLIFIED SPELLING PROPOSALS

(September 25, 1906)

TO THE EDITOR OF THE TIMES

Sir: It is to be regretted that the scheme of the Simplified Spelling Board, so energetically and wisely forced on our attention by President Ruzvelt (if he will allow me to simplify him to that extent) has been received, not only with the outburst of ignorance and folly which any sensible proposal may nowadays count on, but with a false delicacy which has led genuine phonetics experts to withhold serious technical criticism. It is bad enough to have men of letters passionately defending such a recent, absurd, and transient aberration as our pseudo-etymological spelling on the ground that it is the spelling of the Bible and Shakespeare (a libel gross enough to make Tyndale and Shakespeare turn in their graves); but it is far worse to have the defects of the scheme passed over in polite silence by the people who know authoritatively that, though the President does not overrate the enormous importance of spelling reform, his methods cannot be regarded as an advance on those of Artemus Ward and Josh Billings. I tried to express this myself by comparing his action to the reform of the calendar by Mahomed, who divided the year into 12 lunar months, with results on the caravan season arrangements from which Arabian commerce has not recovered to this day. But I find that most of your contemporaries regard Mahomed's arrangement as an excellent one, and accordingly report me as enthusiastically in favor of the Presidential scheme.

Pending some really authoritative comment by Mr. Henry Sweet, whose proposals of 1881 are hardly to the point today, or by some expert of his school, let me point out a few obvious shortcomings in the scheme. To begin with, it is not really a simplified spelling; it is a shortened spelling, which is quite a different matter, as a short spelling may leave a foreigner or a child quite as much in the dark as to the sound of the word as a long one. And it anxiously disclaims any pretence to be phonetic. Now it is doubtless wise, when a reform is introduced, to try to persuade the British public that it is not a reform at all; but appearances must be kept up to some extent at least; and the fact is that a board which disclaims phonetic spelling puts itself out of Court. Unphonetic spelling is as impossible a figment as secular education. Unless we adopt a system of Chinese ideographs, and learn by heart a separate arbitrary symbol of every word in the dictionary we must spell phonetically. We may corrupt and confuse our phonetic spelling by etymologic fads, spelling det with a b and foren with an ig, just as we might spell man mapn or mkyan to show that we are descended from apes or monkeys; but we shall not spell man ape nor shall we ever spell cat dog. If we did the only result would be that we should presently spell dogma catma. We cannot get away from phonetic spelling, because spelling is as necessarily and inevitably phonetic as moisture is damp. To say that English and French spelling are not phonetic is absurd; all that it means is that the French and English spell much worse than the Germans and Italians, being relatively conceited and inhibitive people who take an uppish delight in making knowledge difficult, not to mention their love of excuses for punishing children. English spelling contains thousands of excuses for rebuking children, for beating them, for imprisoning them after school hours, for breaking their spirits with impossible tasks. It is more effective even than teaching a shortsighted child the clock, and then beating it because it cannot tell the time from Big Ben.

But in the long run phonetics have their revenge. When we begin by refusing to spell as we pronounce we end by having to pronounce as we spell. The etymologists, to show the French origin of the word oblige, refused to spell it phonetically; and a generation of superior persons despised those who did not say obleege, and were themselves despised by a still more select circle who said obleezh. But who dares say obleege now, except Joseph Surface on the stage? The history of the word envelope tells the same story. Ongvelope and Ann Velope have had their day; we spelt it ennvelope and now we have to pronounce it ennvelope. The American reformers want us to spell catalogue catalog, a word in such common use that its pronunciation has been traditionally maintained in spite of the spelling. But what of epilog and prolog? These two words, which most Englishmen never utter or hear uttered in their lives, and the rest use perhaps once in 20 years, are on those rare occasions mispronounced, nine times out of ten, as epiloag and proloag. As the working classes become literate and please themselves by dragging into ordinary conversation more and more long words which they have never heard pronounced, they introduce ways of their own of pronouncing them, founded necessarily on the spelling. Programme, a vulgarism which offends the eye as Paris pronounced Paree in English offends the ear, has been in my hearing pronounced so as to rhyme to Damn me. That is how we shall all have to pronounce it some day. I foresee the time when I shall be forced to pronounce semi-conscious as See my Conscious. Then there is the march of preciosity. Already I blush when habit betrays me into calling clothes cloze. I have heard a tenor pronouncing the l in Handel's Where e'er you walk. If Detford has become Depped Ford in spite of usage, I see no reason to doubt that det will presently become debbed. I am fond of the word ham, meaning a country place larger than a hamlet. I am still allowed to speak of East Ham and West Ham, because the words are written separately; but when I speak of Lewis Ham, Elt Ham, or Peters Ham, I am suspected of a defect in my speech, almost as if I had spoken of Cars Halton (properly rhyming to Walton) instead of Ker Shalltn. The received pronunciations nowadays are Louis Sham, Peter Sham, L. Tham, and so on. And the people who support the bad spelling which is corrupting the language in this fashion pretend to have a special regard for it, and prattle of the Bible and Shakespeare! They remind me of a New York Police Commissioner who once arrested a whole theatrical company for performing one of my plays, and explained, on being remonstrated with, that the Sermon on the Mount was good enough for him.

The worst of it is that this want of conscience in spelling has led to anarchy and indifference in the interpretation of spelling. London children are deliberately taught to speak hideously by teachers who speak that way themselves. I have passed a public elementary school and heard a class of children chorusing the alphabet as follows: "I, Ber-ee, Ser-ee, Der-ee, Er-ee, Aff, Jer-ee, Iche, Awy, Ji, Ki, Al, Am, An, Ow, Per-ee, Kioo, Aw, Ass, Ter-ee, Yer-eoo, Ver-ee, Dabblyew, Ax, Wa-eey, Zed." Already the Westend and Oxford have acquired more than half this horrible pronunciation, and they will soon acquire it completely. They are lulled into a false security by the fact that the coarsely nasal resonance of the costermonger distinguishes him socially from the Oxford graduate in spite of the identity of the mispronunciation. But the snarl will no doubt conquer Oxford in time. When smart society says "ow now" for "Oh no" and "dahn-tahn" for "down town" and calls a "humbug with a gun" a "hambag with a gan" it is not very far from complete mastery of the language of what it already calls the Mile End Rowd, and will soon call with native perfection of accent, the Mawl Enn Rowd. Even on the stage young actors are rebuked for speaking as ladies and gentlemen used to speak, and are deliberately taught, not even parvenu English, which is bad enough in all conscience, but positively Hoxton English. The classic beauty of speech by which Mr. Forbes Robertson makes Hamlet still fascinating in spite of its intellectual obsolescence will soon be mimicked (let us hope successfully) as an eccentric dialect; and Mr.——(the name of this excellent actor escapes me for the moment) will perhaps die prematurely, worn out by his efforts to conceal his natural propensity to speak like a gentleman and to acquire the common language of the barrow and the motor-car in all its abhorrent smartness.

I insist on this aspect of the case because, whilst we seem incapable of grasping the enormous advantage of making English a universal language both for writing and speech, or of understanding how our spelling obstructs that consummation, most Englishmen and women would almost rather die than be convicted of speaking like costermongers and flower girls. Our governing classes dropped half the continent of North America from sheer carelessness. Sooner than drop an h they would steep Europe in blood. I therefore hit them purposely in their vulnerable point.

For this very reason, however, the reform cannot be effected by a shortened spelling which is indistinguishable from ordinary wrong spelling. If any man writes me a letter in which through is spelt thru, and above abuv, I shall at once put him down as an illiterate and inconsequent plebeian, no matter what Board or what potentate sanctions his orthography. Really phonetic spelling is quite unmistakeable in this way. No lady or gentleman will ever be persuaded to spell like the late Sir Isaac Pitman, who was a very energetic bookseller and a very bad phonetician; but anybody might spell like Mr. Henry Sweet without compromising himself—indeed with a positive affirmation of having been at Oxford. A practically correct phonetic spelling justified itself at once to the eye as being the spelling of an educated man, whereas the shortenings and so called simplifications suggest nothing but blunders. I therefore respectfully advise the President and the Board to take the bull by the horns without wasting further time, and enlarge the alphabet until our consonants and vowels are for all practical purposes separately represented, and defined by rhyming with words in daily use. We shall then get a word notation which may be strange at first (which does not matter), but which will be neither ludicrous nor apparently ignorant (which does matter very much indeed).

One other point is of importance. The new letters must be designed by an artist with a fully developed sense of beauty in writing and printing. There must be no apostrophes or diacritical signs to spoil the appearance of the pages of the new type. It is a mistake to suppose that the Bible teaches us the sacredness of pseudo-etymological spelling; but it does teach us the comeliness of a page on which there are no apostrophes and no inverted commas.

Yours truly,

G. BERNARD SHAW

Excerpt from *PYGMALION*
and
"PREFACE TO *PYGMALION:* A PROFESSOR OF PHONETICS"
(1912; revised version, 1942)

Millions of people know GBS as the author of the play, *Pygmalion,* on which the musical, *My Fair Lady,* was based. The play, the movie and the musical have been shown in many lands, and translated into many languages.

Similarly, Shaw's writings and activities to popularize alphabet and spelling reform have aroused world-wide interest. The announcement of the bequest in Shaw's Will to use the income of his residual estate to promote alphabet reform of the English language attracted international attention.

Shaw called *Pygmalion* "an advertisement of the science of phonetics." The 1912 version of *Pygmalion* did not include many of the familiar scenes and lines we associate with the musical, *My Fair Lady.* For example, the early version of *Pygmalion* did not contain any scene in which Professor Henry Higgins instructs Eliza Doolittle in the meteorological, phonetic mysteries of "the rain in Spain" that "stays mainly in the plain," or "the *h*urricanes" that "*h*ardly ever *h*appen . . . in *H*ampshire, *H*ereford, and *H*artford." Liza progressed, in *Pygmalion,* from the cockney dialect that restricted her to the life of a "flahr gel" to the supreme test of passing "as a Duchess at an Ambassador's garden party," without the audience even catching a glimpse of the magical process of phonetic instruction that made it all possible. The climactic Garden Party scene of *My Fair Lady* did not appear in the original *Pygmalion,* but was merely alluded to.

Prototypes of these scenes were included in the 1938 movie version of *Pygmalion,* which won an Academy Award. Shaw wrote the scenario himself for the first play he allowed to be made into a full-length, "authorized" movie. GBS inserted new scenes for the edification and "the encouragement of people troubled with accents that cut them off from all high employment." The film included the scene, later incorporated into *My Fair Lady,* in which speech drills are used in the Phonetics Laboratory—with its concealed microphone, large-horned loudspeaker, huge model of a human ear and diagrams of speech organs in various articulatory positions.

The play, *Pygmalion,* opened in London on April 11, 1914, at His Majesty's Theatre. The play had previously been produced in Vienna and Berlin, in German, because Shaw resented earlier criticism of his work and feared the reception the play might receive in England.

In the printed version of the 1912 *Pygmalion,* Shaw represented the cockney dialect of Liza, the Flower Girl, in a transliterated, "phonetic" spelling, just as he had done for the Cockney, Drinkwater, throughout his earlier play, *Captain Brassbound's Conversion,* in 1900. (In 1942, he added the schwa, ə.)

THE FLOWER GIRL. Nah then, Freddy: look wh' y' gowin, deah.

FREDDY. Sorry [*he rushes off*].

THE FLOWER GIRL. [*picking up her scattered flowers and replacing them in the basket*] Theres menners f' yer! Tə-oo banches o voylets trod into the mad.

THE FLOWER GIRL. Ow, eez yə-ooa san, is e? Wal, fewd

dan y' də-ooty bawmz a mather should, eed now bettern to spawl a pore gel's flahrzn than ran awy athaht pyin. Will ye-oo py me f'them? [*Here, with apologies, this desperate attempt to represent her dialect without a phonetic alphabet must be abandoned as unintelligible outside London*].

From that point on, the dialogue of the Flower Girl is written in conventional spelling, except for an occasional onomatopoeic mimicry of Liza's still-developing pronunciation pattern, as in "ye-oo," "whood," "garn," "dunno," or the stereotyping "ah-ah-ah-ow-ow-ow-oo!" This last expletive is used repeatedly as a shibboleth, when Eliza backslides in her articulatory development.

In the scene in which Liza is presented to the Eynsford Hill family, Shaw describes Liza as "speaking with pedantic correctness of pronunciation and great beauty of tone," as "she gasps slightly in making sure of the H in Higgins." But that she is only halfway arrived at cultivated utterance is soon evident in the "new small talk" that Clara finds "delightful and quite innocent." Higgins sardonically comments to Miss Eynsford Hill that she try on every occasion, unselfconsciously, to introduce such quaint locutions as "bloody" and "done-in."

In the 1942 revision of *Pygmalion,* Shaw relied on the more successful movie version. He introduced several entirely new scenes, such as the one in Act II in which Eliza is taught her ABC's, complete with schwa.

Higgins — Say your alphabet.
Liza — I know my alphabet. Do you think I know nothing? I dont need to be taught like a child.
Higgins — (thundering) Say your alphabet.
Pickering — Say it, Miss Doolittle. You will understand

presently. Do what he tells you; and let him teach you in his own way.

Liza — Oh well, if you put it like that–Ahyee, bəyee, cəyee, dəyee–

Higgins — Stop. Listen to this, Pickering. This is what we pay for as elementary education. This unfortunate animal has been locked up for nine years in school at our expense to teach her to speak and read the language of Shakespear and Milton. And the result is Ahyee, Bə-yee, Cə-yee, Dəyee. (To Eliza) Say A, B, C, D.

Liza — But I'm sayin it. Ahyee, Bəyee, Cəyee–

Higgins — Stop. Say a cup of tea.

Liza — A cappətə-ee.

Higgins — Put your tongue forward until it squeezes against the top of your lower teeth. Now say cup.

Liza — C-c-c–I cant. C-Cup.

Pickering — Good. Splendid, Miss Doolittle.

Higgins — By Jupiter, she's done it the first shot. Pickering: we shall make a duchess of her. (To Eliza) Now do you think you could possibly say tea? Not təyee, mind: if you ever say bə-yee cə-yee dəyee again you shall be dragged round the room three times by the hair of your head. T, T, T, T.

Liza — I cant hear no difference cep that it sounds more genteel-like when you say it.

Higgins — Well, if you can hear that difference, what the devil are you crying for? Pickering: give her a chocolate.

Pickering — No, no. Never mind crying a little, Miss Doolittle: you are doing very well; and the lessons wont hurt. I promise you I wont let him drag you round the room by your hair.

Higgins — Be off with you to Mrs. Pearce and tell her about it. Think about it. Try to do it by yourself: and keep your tongue well forward in your mouth instead of trying to roll it up and swallow it. Another lesson at half-past four this afternoon. Away with you.

In Act III, Shaw included a scene at the Embassy Garden Party in which Liza was almost "exposed" as a Hungarian princess of royal blood, obviously not English, because "she speaks English perfectly—too perfectly."

Whiskers — Maestro, maestro. You remember me?

Higgins — No I dont. Who the devil are you?

Whiskers — I am your pupil: your first pupil, your best and greatest pupil. I am little Nepommuck, the marvellous boy. I have made your name famous throughout Europe. You teach me phonetic. You cannot forget ME.

Higgins — Why dont you shave?

Nepommuck— I have not your imposing appearance, your chin, your brow. Nobody notice me when I shave. Now I am famous: they call me Hairy Faced Dick.

Higgins — And what are you doing here among all these swells?

Nepommuck— I am interpreter. I speak 32 languages. I am indispensable at these international parties. You are great cockney specialist: you place a man anywhere in London the moment he open his mouth. I place any man in Europe.

Footman — You are wanted upstairs. Her Excellency cannot understand the Greek gentleman.

Nepommuck— Thank you, yes, immediately. This Greek diplomatist pretends he cannot speak nor understand English. He cannot deceive me. He is the son of a Clerkenwell watchmaker. He speaks English so villainously that he dare not utter a word of it without betraying his origin. I help him to pretend; but I make him pay through the nose. I make them all pay. Ha ha!

Pickering — Is this fellow really an expert? Can he find out Eliza and blackmail her?

Higgins — We shall see. If he finds her out I lose my bet.

Pickering — Well, Eliza, now for it. Are you ready?

Liza — Are you nervous, Colonel?

Pickering — Frightfully. I feel exactly as I felt before my first battle. It's the first time that frightens.

Liza — It is not the first time for me, Colonel. I have done this fifty times—hundreds of times—in my little piggery in Angel Court in my day-dreams. I am in a dream now. Promise me not to let Professor Higgins wake me; for if he does I shall forget everything and talk as I used to in Drury Lane.

Pickering — Not a word, Higgins. Now, ready?

Liza — Ready.

Pickering — Go.

Footman — Miss Doolittle, Colonel Pickering, Professor Higgins.

Hostess — How d'ye do?

Host — How d'ye do? How d'ye do, Pickering?

Liza — How do you do?

Hostess — Is that your adopted daughter, Colonel Pickering? She will make a sensation.

Pickering — Most kind of you to invite her for me.

Hostess — Find out all about her.

Nepommuck— Excellency—

Host — How d'ye do, Higgins? You have a rival here tonight. He introduced himself as your pupil. Is he any good?

Higgins — He can learn a language in a fortnight—knows dozens of them. A sure mark of a fool. As a phonetician, no good whatever.

Hostess — How d'ye do, Professor?

Higgins — How do you do? Fearful bore for you this sort of thing. Forgive my part in it.

Hostess — Ah, here is Professor Higgins; he will tell us. Tell us all about the wonderful young lady, Professor.

Higgins — What wonderful young lady?

Hostess — You know very well. They tell me there has been nothing like her in London since people stood on their chairs to look at Mrs. Langtry.

Hostess — Ah, here you are at last, Nepommuck. Have you found out all about the Doolittle lady?

Nepommuck— I have found out all about her. She is a fraud.

Hostess — A fraud! Oh no.

Nepommuck— YES, yes. She cannot deceive me. Her name cannot be Doolittle.

Higgins — Why?

Nepommuck— Because Doolittle is an English name. And she is not English.

Hostess — Oh, nonsense! She speaks English perfectly.

Nepommuck— Too perfectly. Can you shew me any English woman who speaks English as it should be spoken? Only foreigners who have been taught to speak it speak it well.

Hostess — Certainly she terrified me by the way she said How d'ye do. I had a schoolmistress who talked like that; and I was mortally afraid of her. But if she is not English what is she?

Nepommuck— Hungarian.

All the rest— Hungarian!

Nepommuck— Hungarian. And of royal blood. I am Hungarian. My blood is royal.

Higgins — Did you speak to her in Hungarian?

Nepommuck— I did. She was very clever. She said "Please speak to me in English: I do not understand French." French! She pretend not to know the difference between Hungarian and French. Impossible: she knows both.

Higgins — And the blood royal? How did you find that out?

Nepommuck	–	Instinct, maestro, instinct. Only the Magyar races can produce that air of divine right, those resolute eyes. She is a princess.
Host	–	What do you say, Professor?
Higgins	–	I say an ordinary London girl out of the gutter and taught to speak by an expert. I place her in Drury Lane.
Nepommuck	–	Ha ha ha! Oh, maestro, maestro, you are mad on the subject of cockney dialects. The London gutter is the whole world for you.
Higgins	–	What does your Excellency say?
Hostess	–	Oh, of course I agree with Nepommuck. She must be a princess at least.
Host	–	Not necessarily legitimate, of course. Morganatic perhaps. But that is undoubtedly her class.
Higgins	–	I stick to my opinion.
Hostess	–	Oh, you are incorrigible.
Pickering	–	Where is Eliza? We must keep an eye on her.
Liza	–	I dont think I can bear much more. The people all stare so at me. An old lady has just told me that I speak exactly like Queen Victoria. I am sorry if I have lost your bet. I have done my best; but nothing can make me the same as these people.
Pickering	–	You have not lost it, my dear. You have won it ten times over.

Shaw often repeats the quaint notion that foreigners may speak English better than natives.

The basic theme of *Pygmalion* reflects Shaw's social philosophy, that the potential and life station of a human being should not be conditioned by an unfortunate accident of birth or environment that would be reflected in poor speech.

The science of phonetics can be a liberating force, said Shaw in the didactic "PREFACE TO *PYGMALION:* A PROFESSOR OF PHONETICS," here reprinted in the 1942 revised version, with the new elements in italics.

"Preface to *Pygmalion*: A PROFESSOR OF PHONETICS" (1912; revised edition, 1942)

As will be seen later on, Pygmalion needs, not a preface, but a sequel, which I have supplied in its due place.

The English have no respect for their language, and will not teach their children to speak it. *They cannot spell it because they have nothing to spell it with but an old foreign alphabet of which only the consonants—and not all of them—have any agreed speech value. Consequently no man can teach himself what it should sound like from reading it; and it is impossible for an Englishman to open his mouth without making some other Englishman despise him. Most European languages are now accessible in black and white to foreigners: English and French are not thus accessible even to Englishmen and Frenchmen. The reformer we need most today is an energetic enthusiast: that is why I have made such a one the hero of a popular play.*

There have been heroes of that kind crying in the wilderness for many years past. When I became interested in the subject towards the end of the eighteen-seventies, the illustrious Alexander Melville Bell, the inventor of Visible Speech, had emigrated to Canada, where his son invented the telephone; but Alexander J. Ellis was still a London Patriarch, with an impressive head always covered by a velvet skull cap, for which he would apologize to public meetings in a very courtly manner. He and Tito Pagliardini, another phonetic veteran, were men whom it was impossible to dislike.

Henry Sweet, then a young man, lacked their sweetness of character: he was about as conciliatory to conventional mortals as Ibsen or Samuel Butler. His great ability as a phonetician (he was, I think, the best of them all at his job) would have entitled him to high official recognition, and perhaps enabled him to popularize his subject, but for his Satanic contempt for all academic dignitaries and persons in general who thought more of Greek than of phonetics. Once, in the days when the Imperial Institute rose in South Kensington, and Joseph Chamberlain was booming the Empire, I induced the editor of a leading monthly review to commission an article from Sweet on the imperial importance of his subject. When it arrived, it contained nothing but a savagely derisive attack on a professor of language and literature whose chair Sweet regarded as proper to a phonetic expert only. The article, being libellous, had to be returned as impossible; and I had to renounce my dream of dragging its author into the limelight. When I met him afterwards, for the first time for many years, I found to my astonishment that he, who had been a quite tolerably presentable young man, had actually managed by sheer scorn to alter his personal appearance until he had become a sort of walking repudiation of Oxford and all its traditions. It must have been largely in his own despite that he was squeezed into something called a Readership of phonetics there. The future of phonetics rests probably with his pupils, who all swore by him; but nothing could bring the man himself into any sort of compliance with the university to which he nevertheless clung by divine right in an intensely

Oxonian way. I daresay his papers, if he has left any, include some satires that may be published without too destructive results fifty years hence. He was, I believe, not in the least an illnatured man: very much the opposite, I should say; but he would not suffer fools gladly; *and to him all scholars who were not rabid phoneticians were fools.*

Those who knew him will recognize in my third act the allusion to the *Current Shorthand* in which he used to write postcards. *It may be acquired from a four and sixpenny manual published by the Clarendon Press.* The postcards which Mrs. Higgins describes are such as I have received from Sweet. I would decipher a sound which a cockney would represent by *zerr,* and a Frenchman by *seu,* and then write demanding with some heat what on earth it meant. Sweet, with boundless contempt for my stupidity, would reply that it not only meant but obviously was the word Result, as no other word containing that sound, and capable of making sense with the context, existed in any language spoken on earth. That less expert mortals should require fuller indications was beyond Sweet's patience. Therefore, though the whole point of his Current Shorthand is that it can express every sound in the language perfectly, vowels as well as consonants, and that your hand has to make no stroke except the easy and current ones with which you write m, n, and u, l, p, and q, scribbling them at whatever angle comes easiest to you, his unfortunate determination to make this remarkable and quite legible script serve also as a shorthand reduced it in his own practice to the most inscrutable of cryptograms. His true objective was the provision of a full, accurate, legible script for our language; but he was led past that by his contempt for the popular Pitman system of shorthand, which he called the Pitfall system. The triumph of Pitman was a triumph of business organization: there was a weekly paper to persuade you to learn Pitman: there were cheap textbooks and exercise books and transcripts of speeches for you to copy, and schools where experienced teachers coached you up to the necessary proficiency. Sweet could not organize his market in that fashion. He might as well have been the Sybil who tore up the leaves of prophecy that nobody would attend to. The four and sixpenny manual, mostly in his lithographed handwriting, that was never vulgarly advertized, may perhaps some day be taken up by a syndicate and pushed upon the public as The Times pushed the Encyclopaedia Britannica; but until then it will certainly not prevail against Pitman. I have bought three copies of it during my lifetime; and I am informed by the publishers that its cloistered existence is still a steady and healthy one. I actually learned the system two several times; and yet the shorthand in which I am writing these lines is Pitman's. And the reason is, that my secretary cannot transcribe Sweet, having been perforce taught in the schools of Pitman. *In America I could use the commercially organized Gregg shorthand, which has taken a hint from Sweet by making its letters writable (current, Sweet would have called them) instead of having to be geometrically drawn like Pitman's; but all these systems, including Sweet's, are spoilt by making them available for verbatim reporting, in which com-*

plete and exact spelling and word division are impossible. A complete and exact phonetic script is neither practicable nor necessary for ordinary use but if we enlarge our alphabet to the Russian size, and make our spelling as phonetic as Spanish, the advance will be prodigious.

Pygmalion Higgins is not a portrait of Sweet, to whom the adventure of Eliza Doolittle would have been impossible; still, as will be seen, there are touches of Sweet in the play. With Higgins's physique and temperament Sweet might have set the Thames on fire. As it was, he impressed himself professionally on Europe to an extent that made his comparative personal obscurity, and the failure of Oxford to do justice to his eminence, a puzzle to foreign specialists in his subject. I do not blame Oxford, because I think Oxford is quite right in demanding a certain social amenity from its nurslings (heaven knows it is not exorbitant in its *requirement*!); for although I well know how hard it is for a man of genius with a seriously underrated subject to maintain serene and kindly relations with the men who underrate it, and who keep all the best places for less important subjects which they profess without originality and sometimes without much capacity for them, still, if he overwhelms them with wrath and disdain, he cannot expect them to heap honors on him.

Of the later generation of phoneticians I know little. Among them towered *Robert Bridges* to whom perhaps Higgins may owe his Miltonic sympathies, though here again I must disclaim all portraiture. But if the play makes the public aware that there are such people as phoneticians, and that they are among the most important people in England at present, it will serve its turn.

I wish to boast that Pygmalion has been an extremely successful play *both on stage and screen,* all over Europe and North America as well as at home. It is so intensely and deliberately didactic, and its subject is esteemed so dry, that I delight in throwing it at the heads of the wiseacres who repeat the parrot cry that art should never be didactic. It goes to prove my contention that *great* art *can* never be anything else.

Finally, and for the encouragement of people troubled with accents that cut them off from all high employment, I may add that the change wrought by Professor Higgins in the flower-girl is neither impossible nor uncommon. The modern concierge's daughter who fulfills her ambition by playing the Queen of Spain in Ruy Blas at the Théâtre Français is only one of the many thousands of men and women who have sloughed off their native dialects and acquired a new tongue. *Our West End shop assistants and domestic servants are bilingual.* But the thing has to be done scientifically, or the last state of the aspirant may be worse than the first. An honest slum dialect is more tolerable than the attempts of phonetically untaught persons to imitate *the plutocracy. Ambitious flower-girls who read this play must not imagine that they can pass themselves off as fine ladies by untutored imitation. They must learn their alphabet over again, and differently, from a phonetic expert. Imitation will only make them ridiculous.*

NOTE FOR TECHNICIANS. *A complete representation of the play as printed in this edition is technically possible only on the cinema screen or on stages furnished with exceptionally elaborate machinery. For ordinary theatrical use the scenes separated by rows of asterisks are to be omitted.*

In the dialogue an e upside down indicates the indefinite vowel, sometimes called obscure or neutral, for which, though it is one of the commonest sounds in English speech, our wretched alphabet has no letter.

"SPOKEN ENGLISH and BROKEN ENGLISH"

Script of recordings, in a brochure issued by the Linguaphone Institute (1928)

Shaw's bearded countenance became well known throughout the world during his lifetime through widely distributed picture likenesses of the hirsute playwright. His voice and speech were not equally familiar, despite his many appearances as a public speaker and on the "wireless." Sound film clips have preserved the image and speech of Shaw.

In 1928, the Linguaphone Institute invited Shaw to make a recording of his voice and speech. GBS wrote his own script in which he discussed a favorite subject, the English language, and how to speak it.

The Linguaphone editor said, in the Preface to the brochure containing Shaw's text:

> In every country in the world in which literature holds a place, the name of George Bernard Shaw is well known and, one may say, revered. No other writer, except, perhaps, Shakespeare, has earned such world-wide fame. The portraits broadcast by the press have made his features familiar to millions all over the earth. His writings have been translated into the language of every civilised nation, and there can hardly be anywhere a theatre of any importance at which at least some of his plays have not been

produced. But of the multitudes who have thus become familiar with his name, his features and his work, how many have actually heard the living voice of the man himself? Their number is, comparatively speaking, infinitesimal. Thanks, however, to Mr. Shaw's courtesy in consenting to have his voice reproduced on Linguaphone records, it will now be possible for millions the world over to listen to his voice in their own homes and at their own pleasure.

That it is a great privilege for the Linguaphone Institute to be able to record the voice of this literary genius goes without saying, but, apart from that, the fact that the voice of the Master has thus been perpetuated will be of the utmost interest and importance to the vast number of people who have been entranced by his writings. There has been in modern times no writer who has ever captured the imagination of the public to such an extent as has George Bernard Shaw, and the making of these records represents a boon to his admirers all over the globe and an epoch-making event in the history of literature.

Mr. Shaw very kindly prepared a special address for the recording, and the text of that address composed in his own inimitable style and full of true "Shavian" humor and whimsicality, will be found in the following pages, together with a short sketch of his career.

This is the first time that the voice of a writer of Mr. Shaw's calibre has been recorded, and we deeply appreciate the honour which he has done to the Linguaphone Institute by selecting it as the most appropriate medium through which to record his voice for the benefit of this and future generations.

The text Shaw prepared and spoke on the "gramophone" recording was loaded with characteristic Shavian wit, but with serious purpose behind it all. The provocative ideas were couched in a simple but sparkling rhetorical style.

SPOKEN ENGLISH AND BROKEN ENGLISH
by BERNARD SHAW

(Linguaphone Institute, 1928)

In "Record No. 1," GBS alerted his listeners to the fact that voice and speech, like ideas, can be distorted in the process of being recorded, transcribed and reproduced. He urged listeners to find the proper speed for playing the record, so that it would sound authentic and faithful to the original.

To make his point, GBS used a curious figure of speech in identifying a speaker: "I know his voice as well as I know my own." Shaw must have known how strange one's voice sounds when first heard on a recording.

Record No. 1

Let me introduce myself: Bernard Shaw.

I am asked to give you a specimen of spoken English; but first let me give you a warning. You think you are hearing my voice; but unless you know how to use your gramophone properly, what you are hearing may be something grotesquely unlike any sound that has ever come from my lips.

A few days ago I heard a gramophone record of a speech by Mr. Ramsay MacDonald, the Parliamentary Chief of the British Labour Party, who has a fine, deep Scottish voice and a remarkably musical and dignified delivery. What I heard was a high-pitched, sharp, cackling voice, most unmusical, suggesting a small, egotistical, very ill-mannered man, complaining of something. I said "That is not Mr. MacDonald. I know his voice as well as I know my own." The gramophone operator assured me that it was, and showed me the label on the record to prove it. I said, "No: that is not Ramsay MacDonald; but let me see whether I cannot find him for you." Then, as the record started again, I took the screw which regulates the speed and slowed the record down gradually until the high-pitched yapping changed to the deep tones of Mr. MacDonald's voice; and the unmusical, quarrelsome self-assertion became the melodious rhetoric of the Scottish orator. "There!" I said: "that is Mr. MacDonald."

So you see, what you are hearing now is not my voice unless your gramophone is turning at exactly the right speed. I have records of famous singers and speakers who are dead, but whose voices I can remember quite well: Adelina Patti, Sarah Bernhardt, Charles Stanley, Caruso, Tamagno; but they sound quite horrible and silly until I have found the right speed for them, as I found it for Mr. MacDonald.

Now, the worst of it is that I cannot tell you how to find the right speed for *me*. Those of you who have heard me speak, either face to face with me or over the wireless, will have no difficulty. You have just to change the speed until you recognize the voice you remember. But what are you to do if you have never heard me? Well, I can give you a hint that will help you. If what you hear is very disappointing, and you feel instinctively "that must be a horrid man," you may be quite sure the speed is wrong. Slow it down until you feel that you are listening to an amiable old gentleman of seventy-one with a rather pleasant Irish voice, then that is me. All the other people whom you hear at the other speeds are impostors: sham Shaws! Phantoms who never existed.

In "Record No. 2," Shaw discussed the importance of learning to speak well. He suggested that there are many presentable standards, all equally acceptable so long as they are intelligible and "stamp the speaker as a cultivated person as distinguished from an ignorant and illiterate one."

Record No. 2

I am now going to suppose that you are a foreign student of the English language; and that you desire to speak it well enough to be understood when you travel in the British Commonwealth or in America, or when you meet a native of those countries. Or it may be that you are yourself a native but that you speak in a provincial or cockney dialect of which you are a little ashamed, or which perhaps prevents you from obtaining some employment which is open to those only who speak what is called "correct English." Now, whether you are a foreigner or a native, the first thing I must impress on you is that there is no such thing as ideally correct English. No two British subjects speak exactly alike. I am a member of a committee established by the British Broadcasting Corporation for the purpose of deciding how the utterances of speakers employed by the Corporation should be pronounced in order that they should be a model of correct English speech for the British Islands. All the members of that Committee are educated persons whose speech would pass as correct and refined in any society or any employment in London. Our chairman is the Poet Laureate, who is not only an artist whose materials are the sounds of spoken English, but a specialist in their pronunciation. One of our members is Sir Johnston Forbes-Robertson, famous not only as an actor but for the beauty of his speech. I was selected for service on the Committee because, as a writer of plays, I am accustomed to superintend their rehearsals and to listen critically to the way in which they are spoken by actors who are by profession trained speakers (being myself a public speaker of long experience). That committee knows as much as anyone knows about English speech; and yet its members do not agree as to the pronunciation of some of the simplest and commonest words in the English language. The two simplest and commonest words in any language are "yes" and "no." But no two members of the committee pronounce them exactly alike. All that can be said is that every member pronounces them in such a way that they would not only be intelligible in every English-speaking country, but would stamp the speaker as a cultivated person as distinguished from an ignorant and illiterate one. You will say, "Well: that is good enough for me: that is how I desire to speak." But which member of the committee will you take for your model? There are Irish members, Scottish members, Welsh members, Oxford University members, American members: all recognizable as such by their differences of speech. They differ also according to the county in which they were born. Now, as they all speak differently, it is nonsense to say that they all speak correctly. All we can claim is that they all speak presentably, and that if you speak as they do, you will be understood in any English-speaking country and accepted as a person of good social standing. I wish I could offer you your choice among them as a model; but for the moment I am afraid you must put up with me—an Irishman.

In "Record No. 3," Shaw made the point that we should adjust our speech style to the occasion, a sound observation in line with orthodox rhetorical theory.

Record No. 3

I have said enough to you about the fact that no two native speakers of English speak it alike; but perhaps you are clever enough to ask me whether I myself speak it in the same way.

I must confess at once that I do not. Nobody does. I am at present speaking to an audience of many thousands of gramophonists, many of whom are trying hard to follow my words, syllable by syllable. If I were to speak to you as carelessly as I speak to my wife at home, this record would be useless; and if I were to speak to my wife at home as carefully as I am speaking to you, she would think that I was going mad.

As a public speaker I have to take care that every word I say is heard distinctly at the far end of large halls containing thousands of people. But at home, when I have to consider only my wife sitting within six feet of me at breakfast, I take so little pains with my speech that very often, instead of giving me the expected answer, she says "Don't mumble; and don't turn your head away when you speak. I can't hear a word you are saying." And she also is a little careless. Sometimes I have to say "What?" two or three times during our meal; and she suspects me of growing deafer and deafer, though she does not say so, because, as I am now over seventy, it might be true.

No doubt I ought to speak to my wife as carefully as I should speak to a queen, and she to me as carefully as she would speak to a king. We ought to; but we don't. ("Don't," by the way, is short for "do not.")

We all have company manners and home manners. If you were to call on a strange family and to listen through the keyhole—not that I would suggest for a moment that you are capable of doing such a very unladylike or ungentlemanlike thing; but still—if, in your enthusiasm for studying languages you could bring yourself to do it just for a few seconds to hear how a family speak to one another when there is nobody else listening to them, and then walk into the room and hear how very differently they speak in your presence, the change would surprise you. Even when our home manners are as good as our company manners—and of course they ought to be much better—they are always different; and the difference is greater in speech than in anything else.

Suppose I forget to wind my watch, and it stops, I have to ask somebody to tell me the time. If I ask a stranger, I say "What o'clock is it?" The stranger hears every syllable distinctly. But if I ask my wife, all she hears is "cloxst." That is good enough for her; but it would not be good enough for you. So I am speaking to you now much more carefully than I speak to her; but please don't tell her!

In "Record No. 4," Shaw mixed perception with whimsy—as he put in a plug for "broken English," to round off the spoken English. He urged foreigners not to try to speak English perfectly, lest no native understand them. (This was an idea that Shaw first proposed in *Pygmalion.*)

Though it is sometimes difficult to tell whether GBS was speaking, and writing, with tongue in cheek, the basic theses expressed in *Pygmalion* and in "English and American Dialects" in "Notes to *Captain Brassbound's Conversion*" are reiterated by Shaw in these recordings.

Record No. 4

I am now going to address myself especially to my foreign hearers. I have to give them another warning of quite a different kind. If you are learning English because you intend to travel in England and wish to be understood there, do not try to speak English perfectly, because, if you do, no one will understand you. I have already explained that though there is no such thing as perfectly correct English, there is presentable English which we call "Good English"; but in London nine hundred and ninety nine out of every thousand people not only speak bad English but speak even that very badly. You may say that even if they do not speak English well themselves they can at least understand it when it is well spoken. They can when the speaker is

English; but when the speaker is a foreigner, the better he speaks, the harder it is to understand him. No foreigner can ever stress the syllables and make the voice rise and fall in question and answer, assertion and denial, in refusal and consent, in enquiry or information, exactly as a native does. Therefore the first thing you have to do is to speak with a strong foreign accent, and speak broken English: that is, English without any grammar. Then every English person to whom you speak will at once know that you are a foreigner, and try to understand you and be ready to help you. He will not expect you to be polite and to use elaborate grammatical phrases. He will be interested in you because you are a foreigner, and pleased by his cleverness in making out your meaning and being able to tell you what you want to know. If you say "Will you have the goodness, Sir, to direct me to the railway terminus at Charing Cross," pronouncing all the vowels and consonants beautifully, he will not understand you, and will suspect you of being a beggar or a confidence trickster. But if you shout, "Please! Charing Cross! Which way!" you will have no difficulty. Half a dozen people will immediately overwhelm you with directions.

Even in private intercourse with cultivated people you must not speak too well. Apply this to your attempts to learn foreign languages, and never try to speak them too well. And do not be afraid to travel. You will be surprised to find how little you need to know or how badly you may pronounce. Even among English people, to speak too well is a pedantic affectation. In a foreigner it is something worse than an affectation: it is an insult to the native who cannot understand his own language when it is too well spoken. That is all I can tell you: the record will hold no more. Good-bye!

"A KING'S SPELLING: LETTERS AND SOUNDS"

Letter to *The Times* of London (April 15, 1941)

Shaw's logical temperament was outraged by the irrational spelling of English. He attributed to its vagaries "colossal" waste of labor in printing, writing and education. "No British Government will ever be stirred to action in the matter until the economics of a phonetically spelt scientific and scholarly Pidgin are calculated and stated in terms of time, labour, and money."

Consequently, he advocated an alphabet-spelling reform. He warned of the advantage the Russians enjoyed in the "race of civilization," because they could, in their 35 letter Cyrillic alphabet, spell Shaw with two letters; "but I have to spell it with four letters: another 100 per cent loss of time, labour, ink, and paper. . . . What chance has a Power that cannot spell so simple a sound as Shaw against a rival that can?"

Shaw said, during England's finest hour in World War II: "Battles may be lost by the waste in writing Army orders and dispatches with multitudes of superfluous letters." He asked: "How many wars will it take to call our attention to the fact that there are shorter ways of spelling enuf than e-n-o-u-g-h?" He pointed to the extravagance of wasting 11 letters on "should" and "would," when 6 symbols could do, with a rational system of orthography, or better yet, a new alphabet.

GBS first instructed the reader in phonetics, phonemics and the facts of life about English spelling. Then, in typically didactic Shavian vein, GBS managed a good word for "the phonetist,

Henry Sweet," Basic English, and Pitman's shorthand. His own remedy remained unequivocal: what the English-speaking world needed was a new alphabet.

A KING'S SPELLING
LETTERS AND SOUNDS
(April 15, 1941)

TO THE EDITOR OF THE TIMES

Sir,—I am shocked by the levity and *lèse-majesté* of the leading article "A King's Spelling" in your issue of March 28. You have failed to appreciate either the gravity of the subject or the laudable and sensible attempts of our Sovereign's royal father to spell the English language as it ought to be spelt.

He was, however, attempting the impossible. The English language cannot be spelt, because there is no English alphabet. We make shift with a Latin alphabet which has only five vowels. The vowels we use, mostly diphthongs, are innumerable: no two inhabitants of these isles use the same set; but the sounds they utter are so far recognizably alike as to be intelligibly represented by 18 letters. The consonants, as to which there is much less difference of utterance, require 24 letters.

Our attempts to make a foreign alphabet of 26 letters do the work of 42 are pitiable. We write the same vowel twice to give it a different sound, and thus get five additional vowels. We couple two different vowels, or even triple them, in various permutations, which give us much more than 18 vowel spellings. We also double the following consonant (compare "table" and "dabble," for instance) or make two consonants represent simple sounds like the consonants in "thee" and "she," for which the Latin alphabet does not provide.

These devices would make our alphabet phonetic enough for practical purposes if we used them consistently; but as our use of them is not consistent no one can pronounce a line of English from English writing or print. Still, it may be said that all we have to do is to make our usage consistent and the problem of spelling is solved. Those who think this a satisfactory solution overlook the stupendous fact that it takes twice as long to write two letters as to write one. When it is pointed out to them they protest that the fact is perfectly obvious to them. But stupendous! How? Why? Could any fact be more trivial?

Let us see. The issue of *The Times* in which the article headed "A King's Spelling" appeared was reduced by the war rationing of paper to half the usual size. The leader page, including the article, contained 54,369 letters. Each of the pages in the smaller type used for advertisements contained 88,200 letters. As there were 10 pages we have to multiply these figures by 10. Averaging them we get 712,845 letters as the content of a typical war-rationed 10-page issue of *The Times*. For a normal peace issue of *The Times* we must more than double this figure, which means that every 24 hours in the office of *The Times* alone a million and a half letters must be separately and legibly written or typed on paper, that someone reading from the paper must monotype them on a machine which arranges and casts them in metal, to be finally printed on huge rolls of paper by another machine the wear and tear of which is in proportion to the area of paper covered by the letters. This colossal labour has to be repeated every working day in the year: that is 310 times, which gives us an annual task of writing, setting-up, and printing-off four hundred and sixty-five millions of letters.

This for a single newspaper. But there are the other daily papers, the Sunday papers, the weekly reviews, the magazines, and publications of all sorts, which make the figures astronomical and indeed incalculable. In view of this, what are we to think of our device for making every letter serve two purposes by doubling it? It is easy to say "It takes only a moment to write a letter of the alphabet twice instead of once." In fact it takes years, wears out tons of machinery, uses up square miles of paper and oceans of ink. By shortening a single common word instead of lengthening it, we could save the cost of destroyers enough to make an impregnably guarded avenue across the Atlantic for our trade with America.

It may interest you to learn that your leading article contains 2,761 letters. As these letters represent only 2,311 sounds, 450 of them were superfluous and could have been saved had we a British alphabet. The same rate of waste on the 465,000,000 letters printed annually by *The Times* gives us 94,136,952 superfluous letters, every one of which has to be legibly written or typed, read and set up by the monotypist, cast in metal, and machined on paper which has to be manufactured, transported, and handled. Translate all that into hours of labour at eight hours a day. Translate the labour into wages and salaries. I leave the task to *The Times'* auditors, who, after staggering the proprietors with it, should pass it on to the Auditor-General to be elaborated into an estimate of the waste in the whole printing industry of the nation.

It is, I suppose, for lack of such an estimate that we do not think it worth while to lift a finger to get an English alphabet. The King, who has to spend an appreciable part of his time in signing his name, which in southern English has three sounds, and should be spelt with three letters, has to write six (100 per cent. waste of his time), with a result so equivocal that Herr Hitler speaks of him as King Gay Org. My surname has two sounds; but I have to spell it with four letters: another 100 per cent. loss of time, labour, ink, and paper. The Russians can spell it with two letters, as they have an alphabet of 35 letters. In the race of civilization, what chance has a Power that cannot spell so simple a sound as Shaw against a rival that can?

At present we are in such pressing need of more manpower that we are driven to transfer our women from their special natural labour of creating life to the industry of destroying it. I wonder some female mathematician does not calculate how many men would be released from literary industry for war work by spelling the common words could and should with six letters instead of with 11 as we insanely do at present. Battles may be lost by the waste in writing Army orders and dispatches with multitudes of superfluous leters. The mathematicians changed from Latin numerals to Arabic years ago. The gain was incalculably enormous. A change from Latin to British letters would have equally incalculable advantages; but we, being incorrigibly brain lazy, just laugh at spelling reformers as silly cranks. It took the Four Years' War to knock Summer Time into us. How many wars will it take to call our attention to the fact that there are shorter ways of spelling enuf than e-n-o-u-g-h?

Unfortunately, as most people write little and seldom, and read and spell by visual memory, not aurally, they are unconscious of any serious difficulty, and are only amused when some spelling reformer treats them to a few stale pleasantries about Frenchmen who, having been taught how to pronounce such a monstrosity as the spelling of though (six letters for two sounds), are then left to infer the pronunciation of through, cough, plough, &c., &c. We have endless exposures of the inconsistencies of our spelling and the absurdity of its pretence to etymology; but even professional writers who waste half their lives in blackening paper unnecessarily seem to have no grasp of the importance of our losses or the colossal figures into which they run.

Much work has already been done on the subject by inventors of phonetic shorthands, who have all had to begin by designing a 42-letter alphabet. The best of these, so far as I know, is that of our most eminent British phonetist, the late Henry Sweet, who had mastered all the systems, from Bell's Visible Speech to Pitman's; but, like all the rest, he proceeded to torture it into an instrument for verbatim reporting, and thereby made it difficult to learn, illegible, and useless for ordinary purposes. However, it is easy to discard his reporting contractions and use his alphabet in its simplicity. In my own practice I use Pitman's alphabet in this way with a great saving of time and labour for myself personally; but it all has to be transcribed and set up in the spelling of Dr. Johnson's dictionary.

The Orthological Institute has done invaluable service in calling attention to our waste of time by too much grammar through its invention of Basic English; but though the interest for foreign students is great, no British Government will ever be stirred to action in the matter until the economics of a phonetically spelt scientific and scholarly Pidgin are calculated and stated in terms of time, labour, and money.

Yours truly,

G. BERNARD SHAW

Ayot St. Lawrence, Welwyn, Herts.

"THE AUTHOR AS MANUAL LABORER"

The Author (Summer, 1944)

In this essay, Shaw addressed the perfect audience, in the sense that the argument should have been most congenial to their needs. GBS espoused a new English alphabet for labor-saving purposes for the *writer*. He cited the economic motives of husbanding the writing-time of his fellow scriveners, by suggesting how much effort could have been spared by Dickens and Shakespeare if the language had been spelled rationally and without excrescent letters.

Shaw stated that under no circumstances would he do the specifics himself of devising the new alphabet. He concluded plaintively that since his previous appeals had fallen on deaf ears, he was planning to make a testamentary bequest to launch the enterprise.

[The article that follows in this anthology, "From Bernard Shaw," was originally appended to the present piece in *The Author*—but was later printed separately as a brochure and widely distributed. It was in connection with that public declaration that Sir James Pitman and Professor Daniel Jones visited Shaw at Ayot St. Lawrence in 1947—the meeting with the "great man" that Sir James describes in the "Foreword" to this book.]

"THE AUTHOR AS MANUAL LABORER"

The Author (Summer, 1944)

One would suppose that authors, as they make their living by writing, would be much more keenly interested in labor-saving devices in their trade than artisans and laborers. The author, owning his raw material (paper), his tool (the pen), and his machinery (the typewriter), gains by every invention that saves time and labor in production of copy for the printer. And the right to publish it is his absolute monopoly. The artisan, being a hired operative owning neither raw material nor machinery nor product, is threatened by every improvement in process or machinery with reduction to the rank and wages of an unskilled laborer; and the laborer is thrown out of employment altogether by it. The author, if he had any economic sense or mathematical faculty (mostly he has neither, and is nothing but an artist) would be intensely interested in every chance of shortening his working hours or making them more productive. Yet he seldom gives them a thought except when he thinks it funny to deride them, whilst the artisans and laborers, individually and through their unions, are continually agitated about them. Of course there are exceptions: all authors are not lost when they leave their imaginary worlds for the real one; but in the lump it is notable that scriptorial reforms receive hardly any support from authors, and rather too much from Utopian cranks.

The basic difficulty in writing English is that we have no British alphabet in general use. Our ancient Phoenician alphabet has only 26 letters, whereas the least we need are 42. There are only five vowel sounds to represent the speech of millions of Britishers whose vowels are as different as their finger prints. But as the differences are not wide enough to make Yorkshire unintelligible to Somerset, or Trinity College, Dublin, to Oxford University, it is found in practice that a dozen or so of vowel symbols are quite sufficient to make English writing as intelligible as English speech. There is no need to distinguish between the vowel sounds in *to, too* and *two,* nor between *city* by itself and as it occurs in *publicity.* All British readers will understand without cutting it as fine as that, which reminds me that Robert Bridges would have spelt the last pronoun *thatt.*

But Bridges made this distinction by using two letters for a single sound instead of one; and this meant a colossal addition to the manual drudgery of writing. It seems at first that the time lost by writing *tt* instead of *t* is negligible; but this depends on the number of times you have to write it. Just count the number of *ts* I have had to write since I began this article. Then think of the number of *ts* in this morning's *Times.* Include all the other newspapers in the British Commonwealth and the U.S.A. Add the *ts* in all the books, letters, and documents of every sort that are being written during the current 24 hours. The figure becomes monstrous. Multiply it by 313 to arrive at its amount for all the working days in the year. It becomes astronomical. Bridges was proposing, not the expenditure of a fraction of a second of time, but the cost of a war. And *t* is not the letter we have to write oftenest. Substitute *e,* and double it, as we do to spell *keep* or the American *Gee;* and human imagination staggers at the sum.

Yet it is only by doubling letters or writing one sound with two letters and in different order that we can make our Phoenician alphabet spell English. By resorting to these permutations we have tried to do it; but we have not tried consistently. To spell *receive* and *believe* we have to think of the unpleasant word *lice*. Such consonants as *sh, zh, th, dh* we simply cannot spell at all, and find ourselves calling *Lewis Ham* Louis Sham and *Cars Halton* Car Shallton for want of a symbol to write the first consonant of my name.

As to spelling the very frequent word *though* with six letters instead of two, it is impossible to discuss it, as it is outside the range of common sanity. In comparison such a monstrosity as *phlegm* for flem is merely disgusting.

No author in his senses, having grasped the figures, would use the Phoenician alphabet if a British phonetic one were available. I wish some person with a mania for arithmetic would count the sounds in Shakespear's plays or Dickens's novels, and then count the letters these unfortunate scribes had to write to make readable manuscripts of them for the players and printers. I would burn all the commentaries and criticisms that have been wasted on their works for such a cast-up. It would prove that they in their short lives (I have lived nearly twenty years longer than either of them) could have written two or three more plays and novels than they had time to get through. Shakespear's signatures shew that he suffered from writer's cramp. How his actors read their parts (unless he dictated them to scriveners) is a wonder.

The case of Dickens is extraordinary. He began as a Parliamentary reporter, and had learnt and mastered Gurney's shorthand. Yet he had to write all his novels in Phoenician longhand because his shorthand was legible by nobody but himself. Gurney's shorthand can be written legibly and transcribed by specially expert masters of it. But that means many years of practice, beginning with special natural aptitude.

Take my own case. I learnt Pitman's phonetic alphabet in my teens easily in six weeks or thereabouts. Any author can. But I was put off it by the absurd notion that I could not be fully qualified as a shorthand writer until I could report human utterance verbatim, which means writing 150 words a minute. Now this cannot be done by an alphabet. No mortal can *spell* 150 words in 60 seconds, nor even 100. To do this the alphabet must be contracted and contorted and reduced to a code, with all the prepositions and conjunctions and pronouns represented by ticks and dots, and the vowels not represented at all, and seldom even indicated. It ends in each reporter having his own tricks and his own code, illegible to anyone but himself, and not always by himself after his memory of the speech fades. If he has to spell or even to think for a moment he is lost: the speaker has outstripped him.

But what has all this to do with authorship? An author is not a reporter. His writing speed is not 150 words a minute: it is, year in and year out, about 12. He has to think out every sentence, every phrase, before he writes it. Sometimes he has to think about how to spell a word, and, if our ludicrously inconsistent usage baffles him, to write the doubtful letters illegibly and leave the decision to the compositor. Speed of hand is nothing to him: he can make any phonetic alphabet, Pitman or Gregg (now the most generally known in England and America), perfectly legible by writing the words separately at full length with all the necessary vowels and yet beat the Phoenician alphabet by some years of his working life. That is what I have done with Pitman. For over forty years past all my books and plays have been written in Pitman's phonetic alphabet and transcribed into Phoenician by my secretary for the printer. Sometimes, when time presses, I send my shorthand direct to a newspaper where the typists always transcribe it easily.

The time may be at hand when authors will not write at all. They will speak into a dictaphone, when dictaphones become cheap and portable. The dictaphone may even operate the linotype without the intervention of a compositor. But meanwhile the author who can afford a secretary is wasting much of his life in writing or typing in Phoenician longhand.

The reader will now be able to understand the long letter which I have addressed to the public bodies mentioned in it, and to some others as well.

"FROM BERNARD SHAW"

a public letter, printed as a brochure (1944)
originally appended to
"THE AUTHOR AS MANUAL LABORER"
The Author (Summer, 1944)
and letter
The Author (Autumn, 1944)

Written when GBS was 88, this piece stressed the *economics* of the alphabet reform he advocated. Shaw incorporated in the article the arguments and data which were to become the hallmark of the proposals he offered, with increasing urgency, as time went on.

World War II had been raging for five years. Little significant reaction had been stirred by Shaw's earlier writings on alphabet reform. Hence, as will be seen, he stepped up the tempo of his writings and the frequency of his appeals.

Shaw first announced his testamentary intentions in the widely distributed brochure, "From Bernard Shaw." The plan to support financially the development and dissemination of a new English alphabet was later crystallized in his Will. "The scheme is purely economic. Its object is to save time and labor, whether in producing books and newspapers or teaching children to read, write, and speak."

Shaw dismissed all extant schemes of simplified spelling and respelling codes as inadequate for the purpose he had in mind. To replace the conventional ABC's, he proposed the design and promotion of a new alphabet, which would eventually win out, after competition side by side with "Johnsonese," by virtue of its proven greater efficiency.

Shaw recognized the practical and cultural difficulties of shifting to a new alphabet notation. But he declared that economic necessity should override all considerations. "My view is that a change, far from being an economic impossibility, is an economic necessity."

Shaw announced his determination, later carried out, to bequeath his property to a responsible agency for the purpose of carrying out his declared intention. He sought serious applicants to help him achieve his design.

It is hard to understand, in the light of this preliminary writing and the subsequent confirmation in his Will, how anyone can seriously maintain—as some did—that Shaw was "spoofing" in leaving his residual estate for alphabet reform purposes. To the contrary, it would appear that this was a seriously and carefully thought out plan and design, determined in the ripe maturity of years.

From Bernard Shaw

AYOT ST. LAWRENCE
WELWYN, HERTS.

I am at present making my will. As I intend leaving my property, including certain copyrights, the value of which may run into six figures, to the nation for a specified purpose which is outside the routine of any existing Government department, including that of the Public Trustee or the Charity Commissioners, but which aims at the achievement of an immense national economy, I am up against the difficulty of ascertaining which public department or committee, or what learned Society, I should nominate as an executant of my scheme instead of attempting to create a private Trust *ad hoc*.

My particular fad is the saving of labor by the establishment of a fit British alphabet containing at least 42 letters, and thereby capable of noting with sufficient accuracy for recognition all the sounds of spoken English without having to use more than one letter for each sound, which is impossible with the ancient 26 letter Phenician alphabet at present in use.

There are before the public several phonetic alphabets which fulfil this condition, notably those of Pitman in the British Isles and Gregg in the United States of North America. Both have behind them capable business organizations, for lack of which the alphabets of the eminent English phonetician Henry Sweet and others remain practically unknown. But they have been corrupted and spoilt for general use by being taught exclusively as shorthands for verbatim reporting. Phonetic writing can never reach the speed of human utterance; for the contractions, grammalogues, phraseograms and arbitrary dots and dashes and ticks by which verbatim reporters contrive, after years of practice, to report speeches verbatim, are illegible to anyone but the writer, and hardly even to the writer after memory of the utterances has faded. The classical instance is that of Charles Dickens, who, though qualified as a professional reporter by prolonged and irksome study and practice, nevertheless had to write all his novels in the ordinary script to make them legible by the printer. Shorthands as such may be dismissed as useless for general scripture, though their alphabets, if used without contractions, should be examined by all designers of new alphabets.

Beside these shorthands there are in use, in pronouncing dictionaries, and by professional phoneticians and students, ways of making the 26 letter alphabet phonetic. But the notation of our 16 vowels by the five letters *a e i o* and *u* can be done only by using two letters for one sound, and attaching consistent meanings to each permutation. This seems simple and practical because the possible permutations of five letters are far in excess of the number of sounds that need be noted to make a script generally intelligible. Hence we have what is called Simplified Spelling and the spelling of the phonetic textbooks, to say nothing of the attempts of novelists and playwrights to represent the dialects of their characters—of Sam Weller, Caleb Balderstone, Handy Andy, Fluellen and the rest—by grotesque misspellings. My own experience as a playwright in efforts to write modern cockney dialect phonetically with 26 letters has convinced me of its impossibility. Actors who specialize in cockney have had to transcribe my text into conventional spelling before they could study their parts.

My own contribution to the subject, however, has nothing to do with literature as a fine art. On the contrary, I am persuaded that nothing will be done to reform our scripture until its advocates change their ground and admit that the arguments they have been repeating for the last hundred years have produced no considerable result, and are ranked as more or less amusing essays on the curiosities of literature. My special contention is that the matter is one, not for men of letters, professional or dilettanti, but for economists, mathematicians, and statisticians. To any others the inadequacies of our 26 letter alphabet seem trifling, and the cost of a change quite prohibitive. My view is that a change, far from being an economic impossibility, is an economic necessity. The figures in its favor, hitherto uncalculated and unconsidered, are astronomical. That my name, containing two sounds, has to be spelt in our 26 letter alphabet by four letters, or even that the very common word "though," also a two-sound word, should be spelled with six, seems the most negligible of trifles; for what does one name or one word matter? Is the English language, with its established triumphs of "immortal" literature, stored in millions of printed books, and employing a vast machinery of printing presses, and armies of authors, compositors, readers, writers, school teachers, and etymologists, to be upset and made obsolete at enormous expense for a fad called phonetic spelling?

When the question is put in this way the answer is No: contemptuously No.

When it is tackled mathematically the No becomes a clamorous Yes; and the objections are seen to be hot air exhaled by aesthetes who have never counted the prodigious cost of using two letters where one would suffice. To spell Shaw with four letters instead of two, and "though" with six, means to them only a fraction of a second in wasted time. But multiply that fraction by the number of "thoughs" that are printed every day in all the English newspapers in the British Commonwealth and the United States of America—in the books, in the business letters and telegrams, in the private letters, in the military orders; and the fractions of a second suddenly swell into integers of years, of decades, of centuries, costing thousands, tens of thousands and millions. The saving of this colossal waste would pay for the cost of a British alphabet in days, hours, and even minutes. Even the literary upholders of the Phenician alphabet and its fantastic corruption by the etymological craze would begin to see that Shakespear might have written two or three more plays in the time it took him to spell his name with eleven letters instead of seven, "bough" in five instead of two, and so on through much of his vocabulary, though he spelt much more phonetically than Dr. Johnson.

In my own practice I use the phonetic alphabet of Isaac Pitman, writing without reporters' contractions at my speed of authorship, which averages about 1500 words *per day*. It has saved me a prodigious quantity of manual labor, and can be transcribed on a typewriter by anyone who has spent six weeks in learning the Pitman alphabet; but the time it saves is lost again by the typist, the compositor or linotypist or monotypist, the machinist, the paper makers, and the distributing carriers.

In view of this situation I am ready to make a will leaving all my residuary estate to defray the cost of designing and introducing a British alphabet, transliterating the masterpieces of English literature and our school reading books into it and publishing the transliterations, advertising these publications and propagating their desirability, and, always without tampering with the existing alphabet, launching the other in competition with it until one of the two proves the fitter to survive. Official adoption or compulsion must wait upon prevalence: any attempt to begin with them would only prove the political inexperience and incompetence of their advocates. Nevertheless, appropriate State departments may and should undertake and invent improvements in our national scripture just as they do in weights and measures, coinage, postal operations, traffic machinery, military and naval mechanization, building, sanitation, town planning, &c. &c. The rationalizing of our scripture by a native British alphabet may be added to these activities without any fresh legislation or change of policy; but its adoption for official publications and national records, and its tuition in public schools: in short, its virtual enforcement for general use, will not occur until its utility enforces itself. Meanwhile the existing generation must have its literature in the form to which it is accustomed, reading and spelling by visual memory, not by ear. I should strenuously object to have to read, much less write, my own works in a strange script, though I know I should get accustomed to it in a few weeks if I took that trouble.

I must repeat with all possible emphasis that the scheme is purely economic. Its object is to save time and labor, whether in producing books and newspapers or teaching children to read, write, and speak. Its execution must not be directed by a committee of professional literary persons or educational authorities. Such a committee would at once become a conspiracy to defeat the scheme by endless discussions as to whether it should be adopted or not. Only economists as free as possible from literary or pedagogical prejudices, and already convinced of its labor-saving importance, should be given any part in its direction. Artists should be employed only as artist-calligraphers and designers, or consulted as assessors on the aesthetic amenability of the new scripts and types under consideration.

And now comes the difficulty with which I began this letter. I am a citizen desirous of bequeathing my property to the public for public good. If I do so unconditionally this will be easy enough: the Exchequer will "impetticose the gratillity" as conscience money, and use it to pay for the war or to reduce the income tax. But if I earmark it for a specific purpose, as I propose, I am faced with the question of what public ministry or agency I can name as willing and competent to include the fulfillment of my purpose among its functions. The Public Trustee can accept the bequest, collect its revenue, and pay all the personal legacies to relatives and servants and charities with which it must be saddled; but he cannot invent or propagate a new alphabet. What public body can?

The most obvious choice is the British Council. But the Council has just been charged by the Government with the propagation of Basic English; and though Basic English needs an English alphabet as urgently as any other sort of English its acceptance would be seriously retarded if it were presented in a strange script. The two reforms had better be kept separate. One job at a time is enough for the Council, and one novelty enough for the public. Also the opposition of the thoughtlessly customary people who are the enemies of every change should be divided, not combined.

What public organization then, other than the British Council, can conceivably tackle the alphabet? The Board of Works, which has over thirty divisions with various economic functions? The Imperial Economic Committee of the Home Office? The National Service Department of the Ministry of Labor? The Privy Council? The Paper Economy Committee plus the Scientific Advisers Division of the Ministry of Production? The Royal Commission for the exhibition of 1851? The National Savings Committee? The Department of Scientific and Industrial Research? The National Council of Social Service? The Service for Economic Action? Or, among the private organizations for the public benefit, the Carnegie Trust? The Economic Association? The Orthological Institute? The Pilgrim Trust? The Royal Society of Arts? The Mathematical Society? The Statistical Society?

Among the London City Guilds, the Scriveners and the Stationers and Newspaper Makers might establish their usefulness by providing their country with a British alphabet.

Who speaks first? Or last? I beg the favor of a reply, positive or negative.

faithfully

LETTER

The Author (Autumn, 1944)

My appeal for a new British alphabet has been so far a complete failure. Every Government Department to which I have addressed it has replied that that is not its job. The colleges, Trusts, and Societies sing the same song, the few who vary not being in a position to take action. None of them question the importance of the matter, nor fail in distinguished consideration for myself as an author. For this I thank them sincerely.

As it is quite impossible for me to undertake the business myself (inventors of phonetic alphabets please note this) I have decided to empower my executors to accumulate a fund from which they may finance any promising scheme for providing a new phonetic alphabet capable of expressing the forty-two sounds listed by the late Henry Sweet, Oxford Reader of Phonetics, and then publishing and depositing in the leading libraries certain English classics transliterated into the said alphabet.

Failing the achievement of these objects within twenty years from my death (the legal limit of accumulation) the money will go to other public purposes.

G. B. S.

"MR. BERNARD SHAW'S APPEAL FOR A BRITISH ALPHABET"

Printed postcard (September 13, 1944)

Shaw expressed keen disappointment over his failure to get support for his appeal to "existing . . . and relevant agencies to undertake the production of a British alphabet." He neglected to consider the preoccupation of the English-speaking world with its own physical survival in the fateful year 1944, as well as the rather extreme nature of his proposal.

The Simplified Spelling Society of Great Britain might have accepted his offer, had it followed their ideological pattern. But they were committed to a spelling reform using the conventional 26 letter Roman alphabet, and were thereby excluded from consideration by the terms of GBS' declarations.

The leading spokesman for spelling reform in America, Dr. Godfrey Dewey of Lake Placid, N. Y., Secretary of the Simpler Spelling Association, agreed with the British Simplified Spelling Society. Later, in 1955, the British and American organizations agreed on the use of World English Spelling, a system which advocated consistent, phonemic use of the conventional alphabet, employing some digraphs.

Various groups and individuals applauded GBS' objectives but differed with his proposed alphabet reform as the means of achieving them. However, they were unable to persuade him to their way of thinking; and GBS refused to offer his own alphabet design.

In both these notes, GBS detailed his intentions of "bequeathing to the Public Trustee the means of financing any qualified and responsible body" to carry out the steps of "the designing of an alphabet capable of representing at least the 42 sounds of English speech," and "the transliteration and publication" of his own plays in the new characters. This, in essence, came to pass, as did the alternative use of the money for "other public purposes."

Mr. Bernard Shaw's Appeal for a British Alphabet.

(Printed Postcard, September 13, 1944)

My appeal to existing Government Departments, Colleges, Trusts, Societies, and other relevant agencies to undertake the production of a British alphabet has failed. The need has not been questioned; but the replies are to the same effect: try elsewhere: it is not our job. As, having called attention to its enormous economic importance, and offered to aid its implementation financially, I am far too old and preoccupied to take the work in hand myself, I have finished my part in it by bequeathing to the Public Trustee the means of financing any qualified and responsible body, corporate or individual, which will take certain defined steps in its direction. These steps are, in brief, the designing of an alphabet capable of representing at least the 42 sounds of English speech, as listed by the late eminent phonetic expert Henry Sweet, without using more than one letter for each sound, and finally the transliteration and publication of a few English classics, including two of my own plays, in the new characters. Should this bequest have no effect within twenty years following my death, or be made superfluous, as it should be, by government action, my residuary estate will be administered in other public directions.

The matter is now disposed of as far as I am concerned.

G. B. S.

Ayot Saint Lawrence,
Welwyn, Herts.
13/9/1944

"ORTHOGRAPHY OF THE BOMB—SAVE AS YOU SPELL"

Letter to *The Times* of London (Dec. 27, 1945)

Shaw seized every occasion to promote alphabet reform. And each statement became a cumulative summary of the case. He used the discussion about the A-bomb as a springboard for a letter applauding M. P. Follick for placing spelling reform before the House of Commons and offering to endow a University chair in Phonetics. GBS pointed out that only a recognition of the economic follies of present spelling "can move Cabinets to sit up and take notice." GBS referred to himself as "the only phonetician, economist, and man of letters who realizes how much money there is in a British alphabet with which every sound in our speech can be written with one graphic and easily written symbol without even crosses or dots." He went on to assert, with Shavian assuredness: "If the Phenician alphabet were only turned upside down and enlarged by 17 letters from the Greek alphabet, it would soon pay for the war."

If this seemed to verge on acceptance of the International Phonetic Association alphabet as the panacea, GBS later made clear his rejection of any deviation from his new alphabet program. He called those dissidents who disagreed with his proposals "cranks"—and included intransigent "advocates of spelling reform, simplified spelling, universal language and script merchants, reporting shorthand experts, and perfectionists."

ORTHOGRAPHY OF THE BOMB
SAVE AS YOU SPELL

(Dec. 27, 1945)

TO THE EDITOR OF THE TIMES

Sir,—The atomic bomb has kept journalists for many days writing its name many hundreds of times.

The word "bomb" has three simple sounds. The journalists have had to write with four alphabetic signs. The extra sign is entirely senseless, and not only wastes the writer's time, but suggests an absurd mispronunciation of the word, exactly as if the word "gun" were to be spelt "gung." This is a very mild specimen of the time we waste in writing: we have to write the very common word "though," which has two sounds, with six letters. However, as bomb is topical just now its attraction for your readers must excuse its understatement.

The saving of time by omitting the final *b* is usually taken to be 25 per cent.; and this is taken to be 25 per cent. per annum; but we forget the time factor, Einstein's fourth dimension. We ignore the number of cases we are dealing with, and, as the rate per cent. is exactly the same for one case out of two as for billions out of quadrillions, are landed in the wild absurdity of considering it of equal importance to the statesman.

I can scribble the word "bomb" barely legibly 18 times in one minute and "bom" 24 times, saving 25 per cent. per minute by dropping the superfluous *b*. In the British Commonwealth, on which the sun never sets, and in the United States of North America, there are always millions of people continually writing, writing, writing without a moment's intermission. They must sleep, eat, move about, and play, but never all simultaneously: at every moment some of them are writing: say x millions. There are 690½ millions of them; more than quarter the population of the globe. Those who are writing are losing time at the rate of $131{,}400 \times x$ per annum. I leave it to our statisticians to compute x. Even without it the result is staggering enough to justify a raging priority for a British alphabet, no matter what it costs. Including the x, the figures are astronomical.

And yet our phoneticians have made nothing of this. They have wasted a century raising an empty laugh over our spelling of "cough," "laugh," "enough," "though," &c., &c., &c. They have never knocked into our heads the simple fact that a letter saved in spelling is saved not once but millions of times every day. The same is true of the digits of our arithmetical tables. France must owe its present desperate economic predicament largely to its having chosen as its ruler a certain intensely myopic president named Poincaré, who began counting in twopences the francs he had borrowed in tenpences. His brother, a mathematician, should have taught him better.

The matter has at last been brought before Parliament by Mr. Follick, member for Loughborough; but he, too, puts the case only as it was put a hundred years ago by Alexander Ellis, fifty years ago by Henry Sweet, and repeated a thousand times since by generations of phoneticians without producing any political effect whatever. He offers to contribute generously to the endowment of a university chair of phonetics. But there is a very competent professor of phonetics at University College, though his chair is in urgent need of further endowment. Henry Sweet, our super-phonetician, as such demanded the Oxford Chair of literature so furiously that he forced the recalcitrant university to make him at least a reader there. It was a slight to phonetics which he never forgave (he never forgave anything); but it planted the subject academically. Durham University helped. The thing is done. Even if Mr. Follick succeeds in establishing a chair at every university in the kingdom, the immense economy in writer's time, in paper, ink, and wear and tear of machinery which alone can move Cabinets to sit up and take notice, will remain unachieved.

I seem so far to be the only phonetician, economist, and man of letters who realizes how much money there is in a British alphabet with which every sound in our speech can be written with one graphic and easily written symbol without even crosses or dots. If the Phenician alphabet were only turned upside down and enlarged by 17 letters from the Greek alphabet it would soon pay for the war.

I have appealed to every public department whose functions are in any way relevant to take this matter up; but, with the single exception of the scientific workers, they all agree politely that it is important, but not their job. They have other fish to fry. Mr. Winston Churchill recommended Basic English to the attention of the British Council; but everything that can be done for

Basic English has already been done by Mr. Ogden and the Orthological Institute (which Mr. Follick should endow); and it now needs only a phonetic alphabet to equip it for open competition as *lingua franca* in the modern world. If the British Council will not take this up, the Government should create a new council *ad hoc*.

It is useless to appeal to the education authorities. They dare not interfere with Dr. Johnson's monumental misspelling, which is now much more sacred than the creed and the catechism. I suggested to one eminent official educator that children in the elementary schools should be encouraged to spell phonetically as they speak, so that their mispronunciations should be detected and corrected. He replied that the barest hint of such a step would banish him from public life. I quite believe it. I do not propose to meddle with our classic texts, misspelt or rather unspelt as they are: what I desiderate as a professional writer is an alternative alphabet which will save the millions of hours of manual labour now wasted in a sort of devil worship of Dr. Johnson.

I again appeal to the Government as a Labour Government to appoint either directly or through the British Council or some cognate body a committee of economists and statisticians to provide a new British alphabet sufficiently phonetic to enable native speakers of English to be as intelligible to one another on paper as Somerset and Yorkshire, Dublin and Glasgow, are in conversation without writing more than one sign for each sound.

The following is a list of the cranks that must be disqualified from participation at all costs:—

(1) Persons who want to force everybody to spell in

the same way on the ground that their way is right and every other way wrong.

(2) Advocates of spelling reform, simplified spelling, and all attempts to make the Phenician alphabet do the work of a British one. No Englishman will ever have himself set down as illiterate, ignorant, ridiculous, and even occasionally indecent by beginning his epistles with "Deer Sur" and recalling the dying speech of Bombastes Furioso by writing the word "bomb" in simplified spelling.

(3) Universal language and universal script merchants. The ears of a fool are in the ends of the earth; and for a universal script Bell's Visible Speech has been available for a century past. 690½ million people are enough to begin with.

(4) Reporting shorthand experts, who can write 150 words a minute by code without spelling, and assume that the sole object of the new alphabet must be to enable everyone to do the same. Nobody except professional reporters want to do anything of the sort. All my works for 50 years past have been written in Isaac Pitman's phonography. I have to think out and find words and syntax for what I write; and as 1,250 words of such work in two hours or so is enough for a day, my speed, year in and year out, is about 12 words per minute year in and year out. I am neither a reporter nor do I dictate; and a reporting code is as useless to me as a cyclotron. It takes years to acquire. Phonography without reporters' contractions can be acquired in six weeks.

(5) Perfectionists who will not consent to anything that cannot do everything. *Le mieux est l'ennemi du bien.*

(6) The old guard who keep on repeating the arguments of Alexander Ellis and Isaac Pitman and ignoring the economic case which alone can move the Johnsonian mountain.

There are others, but no room for them all here. The phonetics involved are simple A.B.C.: what we need are economically and statistically minded men and women of vision, even if they are hopelessly bad spellers and cannot add up their own washing bills.

Faithfully,

G. BERNARD SHAW

"BERNARD SHAW ON 'OOTOMATIK SPELING'"

Letter to *Tit-Bits* (March 22, 1946)

Shaw commented again in this letter on the proposal for spelling reform legislation offered by Dr. Mont Follick, M. P. from Loughborough. Shaw had previously praised Follick's efforts in a letter to *The Times* of London of December 27, 1945. A seasoned advocate of spelling reform, Follick was chiefly concerned with influencing positively the acceptance of English as an international tongue.

Follick, author of "The Influence of English," had introduced the Spelling Reform Bill to the House of Commons in 1945. He introduced another which was debated on Friday, March 11, 1949, and a third in 1953. In the 1949 debate, Follick called Shaw "that great literary genius, philosopher and cantankerous recluse."

Follick's individualized program deviated from that of the Simplified Spelling Society of Britain, who were not in favor of action on the governmental level at that time. He agreed with them on the principle of the consistent use of the conventional alphabet, with digraphs for certain sounds, but introduced his own variants. In his article in *Tit-Bits,* Follick advocated "Ootomatik Speling," his own simplified orthography.

In his letter of disavowal, GBS observed that "amended orthography" was not effective as a spelling reform because, however phonetic or rational, unconventional orthography in the conventional alphabet connoted illiteracy. "The phonetically spelt texts" seem "ridiculous and even sometimes obscene," wrote Shaw, paraphrasing similar remarks made in 1906 by critics of President Theodore Roosevelt, and later by H. L. Mencken in *The American Language.*

In a 1943 letter to his old friend, Mr. (now Sir James) Pitman, Shaw had said: "Stick to phonetics and economics." In that letter, Shaw stressed the "saving in labor," an observation he repeated in the present comment, and to which he adhered.

BERNARD SHAW On "Ootomatik Speling"

(Letter to *Tit-Bits,* March 22, 1946)

In the previous issue of 'Tit-Bits,' Dr. M. Follick, M.P., advocated Automatic Spelling as a means of furthering understanding among the nations. Many letters were received from readers, and the following is from Mr. George Bernard Shaw:

Everything that Dr. Follick says about our spelling is true; but it was said by Alexander J. Ellis a hundred years ago, and has been repeated again and again by the most eminent phoneticians without producing the smallest effect. The reason is that as so presented the change has seemed enormously expensive and the phonetically spelt texts ridiculous and even sometimes obscene.

What is needed is a new alphabet of not less than 42 letters, which is the lowest number sufficient to represent all the sounds of spoken English recognizable by a single symbol each. Dr. Follick, by confining himself to 22 letters of the present alphabet, is compelled to represent single sounds by several letters, and has landed himself in such monstrosities as "ei tscheir" to spell "a chair"; 9 letters for 3 sounds! I can write "a chair" 12 times in a minute, and "ei tscheir" only 9 times. The number of minutes in a day is 1,440. In a year 525,600! ! !

To realize the annual difference in favor of a forty-two letter phonetic alphabet as against Dr. Follick's Ootomatik alphabet you must multiply by the number of minutes in the year, the number of people in the world who are continuously writing English words, casting types, manufacturing printing and writing machines, by which the total figure will have become so astronomical that you will realize that the cost of spelling even one sound with two letters has cost us centuries of unnecessary labor. A new British 42 letter alphabet would pay for itself a million times over not only in hours but in moments. When this is grasped, all the useless twaddle about enough and cough and laugh and simplified spelling will be dropped, and the economists and statisticians will be set to work to gather in the orthographic Golconda.

Work at the figures for yourself. When you do you will waste no more time in repeating and discussing what has been said exhaustively and quite vainly by a century of phoneticians from Ellis to Dr. Follick. The job of designing the new forty-two letter alphabet is one for the British Council; but it may be done in North America or any of the British Dominions.

Do as much of the propaganda as you can.

G. Bernard Shaw

"COLOSSAL LABOR SAVING: AN OPEN LETTER FROM BERNARD SHAW"

Brochure (May, 1947)

Again, Shaw proclaimed his oft-reiterated thesis that an alphabet reform would save 20% of the working time in the average writer's life span. GBS applied this formula to himself, Shakespeare and Dickens, with staggering results. In this essay, Shaw ranged over the field, rejecting Simplified Spelling, praising the virtues of Pitman's shorthand, proffering "duodecimal arithmetic."

GBS pointed out the dangers of getting bogged down in the niceties of "phonetics" for spelling purposes, lest one seek to identify subtle shades of sound that have nothing to do with the essential purposes of communication. GBS identified "phonemics" as the art of representing symbolically the 44 distinguishable sounds that give intelligibility and meaning to words in the English language. This concept would be useful, he thought, in the new alphabet to be devised for English. Shaw repeated the requirement of beauty and grace in the symbols to be created for the New British Alphabet.

Shaw also turned his attention to the potential international acceptance of a rationally spelled and simplified English language, a concept to which he was apparently belatedly persuaded. He extended his proposal to the logical extreme of applying it to Basic English or some form of Pidgin as a universal language. "And as the sole purpose of speech and writing is to enable us to communicate with one another," he here advocated a language variant of English that enjoyed the complete elimination of grammar and inflected forms.

COLOSSAL LABOR SAVING

AN OPEN LETTER FROM BERNARD SHAW

(May, 1947)

Phone & Wire: AYOT SAINT LAWRENCE,
CODICOTE 218. WELWYN, HERTS.

Simplified Spelling has been advocated for 100 years without producing the smallest effect. To waste another moment on it seems to me perverse indifference to hard fact. People will not accept a spelling that looks illiterate. To spell English phonetically within the limits of a 26 letter alphabet is impossible. A British alphabet must have at least 44 letters; and though the addition of 19 new letters to Dr. Johnson's stock would distinguish it from illiterate spelling the result would not be Simplified Spelling.

What hinders a change is its apparently enormous cost. Only one answer can overcome this hesitation. In any fair and simple test between two experts copying the same text for a minute in Johnsonese and in phonetic, the time saved by phonetic will come out round about 20% as stated by our phoneticians. Such a figure impresses nobody: we might as well attempt to move Mont Blanc with an egg spoon. But the figure is wrong: it leaves out the time factor. We are used to read per cent as per cent per year; but in the test per cent is per cent per minute. Now there are 525,000 minutes in a year; consequently the saving 20% per minute means a labor saving of two months' working days per scribe every year. Multiply this figure by an estimate of the number of persons who at every moment of the 24 hours are writing the English language in the British Commonwealth and in America, and the total is astronomical. The mere suggestion of it is enough to sweep away the notion that we cannot afford the change. On the contrary we cannot afford to postpone it for five minutes.

As far as I know, this overwhelming calculation has never before been presented. I arrived at it by considering the saving of manual labor to myself as an author by using Pitman's phonetic alphabet instead of Johnson's. I have done so for the last fifty years, ever since I could afford a secretary-typist who could read Pitman.

I reflected on the number of plays Shakespear would have had time to write if he had written them in the phonetic alphabets of Pitman, Sweet, or Gregg, and on the staggering fact that Dickens, though a professional verbatim reporter, had to go through the drudgery of writing all his novels in Johnsonese longhand for the printer.

Why could Dickens not have used his shorthand as I used Pitman? Because Pitman, like Sweet and Gregg, corrupted their scripts into codes for verbatim reporting, which is phonetically impossible, as men speak faster than they can write, and therefore have to be reported not by phonetic alphabets but by scrawls on paper which the reporter has come to associate with a few thousand words and phrases after years of practice. Such scrawls vary enough to be illegible by anyone but the reporter, and not always by him or her after the speech fades from memory. You have only to glance at the final chapters of the manuals of Pitman, Sweet, and Gregg to see that their contractions and grammalogues and "word signs" have abandoned all pretence of spelling, and cannot be read, nor even guessed, by readers who know thoroughly the alphabets on which they are founded, and which can be mastered in a month. Sweet, after seven years' work at his shorthand, came to believe that anyone who could not guess a word from a single one of its vowels must be mentally defective. I once received a letter written in it. It took me two months to decipher it, though I knew every letter in Sweet's alphabet.

Shorthand verbatim reporting must therefore be left out of the question. My own speed as an author having to think as I write I estimate at 12 words a minute year in and year out; but to save the manual labor of writing such a sentence as *the kneeling knight thought he knew* with 17 letters instead of 30 I would go to any length. What a phonetic alphabet must save is manual labor, no matter whether it is written at 12 words a minute or 200.

Why not solve the problem as I have solved it for myself by using the existing phonetic alphabets without reporting contractions? They all have the requisite 40-

odd letters. I recommend all authors to do this; but it has all to be rewritten by the typist for the printer in Johnsonese. Besides, they are not graphic enough, not handsome enough, use vertical and horizontal strokes not writable *currente calamo,* and have only a pretence of the sixteen indispensable vowels. A page of the new alphabet should be as handsome as a page set by Jensen or Morris, or a page of the Chantilly psalter. Ugly books would damn any alphabet.

As to teaching children writing and spelling, I urged a Minister of Education to allow and encourage them to spell phonetically just as they speak, which would enable teachers to detect their mispronunciations and correct them. He replied that the slightest hint at such a heresy would banish him from public life. Freedom of spelling should be one of our slogans. If we could carry it into the schools it would at once shew that phonetic spelling is impossible with our alphabet. We must have at least 44 letters, and could do very well with some more for the double consonants.

The advocates of duodecimal arithmetic (mostly also phoneticians) have never used the labor saving argument which alone could move the world to add two new digits for 10 and 11 to our tables. When Poincaré devalued the French franc from tenpence to twopence, it was as if he made the astronomers give up light hours as units and count distances in centimetres; but nobody said a word against this monstrous addition to the manual labor of French accountancy, though there was plenty of protest against the dishonesty of the transaction. Our advantage through counting in pounds is enormous, and would be increased if we changed to duodecimals, compared to which the existing decimal notations are wasteful and inconvenient.

Phoneticians waste time and quarrel over their different plans for a universal language and for correct spelling. Complete phonetic spelling is impossible: Henry Sweet claimed that he could distinguish 11,000 sounds in spoken English; and I, as ex-chairman of the B.B.C. Committee for Spoken English, can testify that no two speakers have the same vowels any more than they have the same finger prints. But an alphabet of 11,000 letters is not necessary. Though we have as many different accents as there are millions of population, we can understand one another's speech and writing with an alphabet of 44 letters without the least difficulty; and as the sole purpose of speech and writing is to enable us to communicate with one another, 44 letters are enough.

There is still the question of foreign languages. Here we assume that it is necessary to write and speak these grammatically. On the contrary, we must abolish grammar to the least practical point. For example, Spanish would be an easy language to learn but for its irregular verbs. But why not regularize them? When a child says "I think you buyed me a doll" it is perfectly intelligible. What more is needed? When an English peasant says "I be, you be, we be, they be" we understand him quite as well as if he said "I am, you are, he is, we are, they are."

Already this simplification is in use in China and Australia as Pidgin, which will probably be the international language of the future. A thousand words of phonetically spelt Basic English, with a positive and negative of Okay and No Can, will make business easy between all nations without declensions, genders, tenses, conjugations, or what we call scholarship. The word pidgin is a Chinese attempt to pronounce our word business; and we owe its spread to the fact that English ousts its over-inflected rivals by its comparative freedom from grammar. What holds it back is the spelling forced on it by a Phenician alphabet with only five vowels instead of sixteen.

However, one thing at a time.

There need be no more discussion about spelling: the required 44 letters are established in all phonetic treatises and scripts. The reform must be conducted by politicians, statisticians, and mathematicians, with, as assessors, printing engineers and possibly an author or two. The new alphabet must be designed by artist-calligraphers.

As there will be immense benefit for everybody without reference to commercial profit or loss, the alphabet is clearly the business of the British Council at the public expense. The Council is now expressly charged with Basic English; but everything that can be done for this has already been done thoroughly by the Orthological Institute, leaving no further action possible except the provision of an alphabet in which Basic English can be intelligibly and economically spelt.

It is a hundred years since the first phoneticians did all they could for Spelling Reform, without the slightest success. The motive power must now come from the colossal labor saving figures, which are new. I have done what I can to draw attention to them; but this is a whole-time-job for a reformer out for a success like that of Rowland Hill; and I, a superannuated playwright and Victorian Fabian sociologist, can only suggest. Perhaps it would suit you.

faithfully

G. B. S.

"A FORTY-LETTER BRITISH ALFABET"

Printed postcard, reprinted in the
Quarterly Journal of Speech (October, 1948)

In this condensation of his ideas, Shaw reduced the number of symbols required for his new "alfabet" from the previously suggested forty-four to forty. In his brief exposition, Shaw deplored the "inconsistency" in "Johnsonese," i.e., spelling in conventional orthography first given sanction by Samuel Johnson's 1755 dictionary.

The rationale for accepting Shaw's proposal combined the economies of a 25% time-saving in writing, added to the reduction in the time in which children might learn to read in the new "alfabet," an idea to which Shaw subscribed on occasion.

At one point, Shaw writes "labour;" at another, "labor." He spells "honor" in the American way, first introduced by Noah Webster, but retains the British "colour"—perhaps to point up the inconsistencies in the international orthography of English.

A Forty-Letter British Alfabet

The number of letters in our Johnsonese alfabet, minus *x, c,* and *q* (unnecessary) is	23
The following consonants are missing: *sh, zh, wh, ch, th, dh,* and *ng*	7
Also missing are the vowels and diphthongs *ah, aw, at, et, it, ot, ut, oot, yoot,* and the neutral second vowel in *colour, labour, honor,* etc.	10
	40

A quite phonetic British alfabet is impossible because the vowels of British speakers differ as their finger prints do; but the 40 sounds listed above will make them as intelligible to one another in writing as they now are in speech. Thus, though Oxford graduates and London costermongers pronounce son and sun as *san* and Ireland as *Awlnd,* they understand one another in conversation.

In Johnsonese the missing letters are indicated by using two or three letters for a single sound. For instance, *though* has six letters for two sounds. A 40-letter alfabet providing one unambiguous symbol for each sound would save manual labor at the rate of 25 per cent per minute (131,400 per annum). Multiply this figure by the millions at every moment busy writing English somewhere in the world, and the total saving is so prodigious that the utmost cost of a change is negligible.

Children, who now have to master the multiplication and pence tables, could learn a 40-letter alfabet easily. Johnsonese is so full of inconsistencies that the few who can spell it do so not by the sound of the word but by the look of it.

Excerpts from the "PREFACE BY GEORGE BERNARD SHAW" to *THE MIRACULOUS BIRTH OF LANGUAGE* by R. A. Wilson (Philosophical Library, New York, 1948)

The New York Times Magazine reprinted a section of the "Preface" to *The Miraculous Birth of Language* on August 20, 1961, using the title, "The Case for Fonetik Speling." *The Times'* introduction stated: "The British are trying a new alphabet in their schools, a matter on which a certain wielder of the English Language (initials G.B.S.) held very lively views."

There is widespread interest in how we can better teach our children to read. An experiment that has attracted wide attention was begun in Great Britain in September, 1961, in which many thousands of British children are involved in learning to read by using an "Initial Teaching" alphabet (I.T.A.). This system, based on phonemic principles, uses 24 symbols of the conventional alphabet, in lower case exclusively, without the letters Q and X; adds nineteen new ligature-symbols, for vowels, diphthongs and consonants for which the Traditional Orthography (T.O.) has no symbol; and thus retains the one sign—one sound phonemic principle. After the children have learned to read in I.T.A., they are transferred to conventionally spelled materials. They seem to learn to read faster and better, in less time.

Sir James Pitman, who wrote the Foreword to this book, is a member of the research foundation supporting this experiment. It is expected to go on for many years to provide a test of the effectiveness of this method of teaching reading. Its proponents feel that children will gain greater confidence and make faster progress. Similar experiments were carried on in St. Louis from 1866 to 1870, and reported to the then "National Educational Association" (NEA) by Dr. Edwin Leigh in 1873. The pioneering ideas of Ellis and Pitman in Great Britain in previous decades called for similar approaches, tried in Waltham, Mass. in the early nineteenth century, and there reported to be successful. Similar research is getting under way in American schools.

* * * *

In undertaking, at the age of 92, to do a Preface to another man's book, George Bernard Shaw again demonstrated the deep seriousness and profundity of his concern with the destiny of the English language. After an abstruse, discursive discussion of Darwinism, morality and the philosophy of science (deleted from the abridged version offered here), Shaw developed his thesis about language and the need for alphabet-spelling reform in English.

The portion of the Preface reprinted here is a good summary of most of GBS' ideas in the field of language.

PREFACE
by George Bernard Shaw
to *The Miraculous Birth of Language*
(1948)

This book by Professor Wilson is one in which I should like everyone to be examined before being certified as educated or eligible for the franchise or for any scientific, religious, legal, or civil employment. My own profession is, technically, that of a master of language; I have been plagued all my life by scientists, clergymen, politicians, and even lawyers, who talk like parrots, repeating words and phrases picked up from one another by ear without a moment's thought about their meaning, and accept mere association of ideas as an easy substitute for logic. They are often good fellows and even clever fellows; but they are not rational. And they are incurably addicted to their personal habits, which they call human nature....

Imagine my delight when I received a copy of the first edition of this book inscribed by its author as "an instalment of interest on an old debt." His name being unknown to me, I hastened to ascertain whether his chair was at Oxford or Cambridge, Owen's or Edinburgh, Dublin or Birmingham. I learnt that it was at Saskatoon, a place of which I had never heard, and that his university was that of Saskatchewan, which was connected in my imagination with ochred and feathered Indians rather than with a university apparently half a century ahead of Cambridge in science and of Oxford in common sense.

Now I had noticed for some years past that American culture, which forty years ago seemed to subsist mentally on stale British literary exports, was more and more challenging our leadership, especially in science. When I learned that provincial Canada had drawn easily ahead of Pasteurized Pavloffed Freudized Europe, and made professors of men who were in the vanguard instead of among the stragglers and camp followers, I found myself considering seriously, especially when the German airmen dropped a bomb near enough to shake my house, whether I had not better end my days in Vancouver, if not in Saskatoon. Meanwhile I urged, as strongly as I could, the reprinting of Professor Wilson's treatise in a modestly priced edition baited for the British book market with a preface by myself: an overrated attraction commercially, but one which still imposes on London publishers.

But I did not look at it commercially. I had an axe of my own to grind; and I thought Professor Wilson's book might help me to grind it. I am not a professor of language: I am a practitioner, concerned with its technique more directly than with its origin. Professor Wilson described how Man was a baby, to whom Time and Space meant no more than the present moment and the few feet in front of his nose, until writable language made Time historical and Thought philosophical. Thought lives on paper by the pen, having devised for itself an immortal and evergrowing body. You will understand this when you have read the book; and I hope you will appreciate its importance, and the magnitude of the service its author has done you.

Meanwhile, where do I come in? Solely as a technician. Professor Wilson has shewn that it was as a reading and writing animal that Man achieved his human eminence above those who are called beasts. Well, it is I and my like who have to do the writing. I have done it professionally for the last sixty years as well as it can be done with a hopelessly inadequate alphabet devised centuries before the English language existed to record another and very different language. Even this alphabet is reduced to absurdity by a foolish orthography based on the notion that the business of spelling is to represent the origin and history of a word instead of its sound and meaning. Thus an intelligent child who is bidden to spell debt, and very properly spells it d-e-t, is caned for not spelling it with a b because Julius Cæsar spelt the Latin word for it with a b.

Now I, being not only a scribe but a dramatic poet and therefore a word musician, cannot write down my word music for lack of an adequate notation. Composers of music have such a notation. Handel could mark his movements as *maestoso,* Beethoven as *mesto*, Elgar as *nobilemente,* Strauss, as *etwas ruhiger, aber trotzdem schwungvoll und enthusiastich.* By writing the words *adagio* or *prestissimo* they can make it impossible for a conductor to mistake a hymn for a hornpipe. They can write *ritardando, accellerando* and *tempo* over this or that passage. But I may have my best scenes ridiculously ruined in performance for want of such indications. A few nights ago I heard a broadcast recital of The Merchant of Venice in which Portia rattled through "How all the other passions fleet to air!" exactly as if she were still chatting with Nerissa and had been told by the producer to get through quickly, as the news had to come on at nine o'clock sharp. If that high spot in her part had been part of an opera composed by Richard Strauss a glance at the score would have saved her from throwing away her finest lines.

These particular instances seem impertinent to Professor Wilson's thesis; but I cite them to shew why, as a technician, I am specially concerned with the fixation of language by the art of writing, and hampered by the imperfections of that art. The Professor's conspectus of the enormous philosophical scope of the subject could not condescend to my petty everyday workshop grievances; but I may as well seize the opportunity to ventilate them, as they concern civilization to an extent which no layman can grasp. So let me without further preamble come down to certain prosaic technical facts of which I have to complain bitterly, and which have never as far as I know been presented in anything like their statistical magnitude and importance.

During the last 60 years I have had to provide for publication many millions of words, involving for me the manual labor of writing, and for the printer the setting up in type, of tens of millions of letters, largely superfluous. To save my own time I have resorted to shorthand, in which the words are spelt phonetically, and the definite and indefinite articles, with all the prepositions, conjunctions and interjections, as well as the auxiliary verbs, are not spelt at all, but indicated by dots and ticks, circles or segments of circles, single strokes of the pen and the like. Commercial correspondence is not always written: it is often spoken into dictaphones which cost more than most private people can afford. But whether it is dictaphoned or written in shorthand it has to be transcribed in ordinary spelling on typewriters, and, if for publication, set up from the typed copy on a printing machine operated by a stroke of the hand for every letter.

When we consider the prodigious total of manual labor on literature, journalism, and commercial correspondence that has to be done every day (a full copy of the London Times when we are at peace and not short of paper may contain a million words) the case for reducing this labor to the lowest possible figure is, for printers and authors, overwhelming, though for lay writers, most of whom write only an occasional private letter, it is negligible. Writers' cramp is a common complaint among authors: it does not trouble blacksmiths.

In what directions can this labor be saved? Two are obvious to anyone interested enough to give half an hour's thought to the subject. 1. Discard useless grammar. 2. Spell phonetically.

Useless grammar is a devastating plague. We who speak English have got rid of a good deal of the grammatic inflections that make Latin and its modern dialects so troublesome to learn. But we still say I am, thou art, he is, with the plurals we are, you are, they are, though our countryfolk, before school teachers perverted their natural wisdom, said I be, thou be, he be, we be, you be, they be. This saved time in writing and was perfectly intelligible in speech. Chinese traders, Negroes, and aboriginal Australians, who have to learn English as a foreign language, simplify it much further, and have thereby established what they call business English, or, as they pronounce it, Pidgin. The Chinese, accustomed to an uninflected monosyllabic language, do not say "I regret that I shall be unable to comply with your request." "Sorry no can" is quite as effective, and saves the time of both parties. When certain Negro slaves in America were oppressed by a lady planter who was very pious and very severe, their remonstrance, if expressed in grammatic English, would have been "If we are to be preached at let us not be flogged also: if we are to be flogged let us not be preached at also." This is correct and elegant but wretchedly feeble. It says in twenty-six words what can be better said in eleven. The Negroes proved this by saying "If preachee preachee: if floggee floggee; but no preachee floggee too." They saved fifteen words of useless grammar, and said what they had to say far more expressively. The economy in words: that is, in time, ink and paper, is enormous. If during my long professional career every thousand words I have written could have been reduced to less than half that number, my working lifetime would have been doubled. Add to this the saving of all the other authors, the scribes, the printers, the paper millers, and the makers of the machines they wear out; and the figures become astronomical.

However, the discarding of verbal inflections to indicate moods, tenses, subjunctives, and accusatives, multiplies words instead of saving them, because their places have to be taken by auxiliaries in such a statement as "By that time I shall have left England." The four words "I shall have left" can be expressed in more inflected languages by a single word. But the multiplication of words in this way greatly facilitates the acquisition of the language by foreigners. In fact, nearly all foreigners who are not professional interpreters or diplomatists, however laboriously they may have learnt classical English in school, soon find when they settle in England that academic correctness is quite unnecessary, and that "broken English," which is a sort of home made pidgin, is quite sufficient for intelligible speech. Instead of laughing at them and mimicking them derisively we should learn from them.

In acquiring a foreign language a great deal of trouble is caused by the irregular verbs. But why learn them? It is easy to regularize them. A child's "I thinked" instead of "I thought" is perfectly intelligible. When anybody says "who" instead of "whom" nobody is the least puzzled. But here we come up against another consideration. "Whom" may be a survival which is already half discarded: but nothing will ever induce an archbishop to say at the lectern "Who hath believed our report? and to who is the arm of the Lord revealed?"

But it is not for the sake of grammar that the superfluous m is retained. To pronounce a vowel we have to make what teachers of singing call a stroke of the glottis. The Germans, with their characteristic thoroughness, do this most conscientiously: they actually seem to like doing it; but the English, who are lazy speakers, grudge doing it once, and flatly refuse to do it twice in succession. The Archbishop says "To whom is" instead of "to who is" for the same reason as the man in the street, instead of saying Maria Ann, says Maria ran. The double *coup de glotte* is too troublesome. No Englishman, clerical or lay, will say "A ass met a obstacle." He says "A nass met a nobstacle." A Frenchman drops the final t in "*s'il vous plaît,*" but pronounces it in "plaît-il?" Euphony and ease of utterance call for such interpolations.

I can give no reason for the Cockney disuse of final l. Shakespear, accustomed to be called Bill by Anne Hathaway, must have been surprised when he came to London to hear himself called Beeyaw, just as I was surprised when I came to London from Ireland to hear milk called meeyock. Final r does not exist in southern

English speech except when it avoids a *coup de glotte*. In that case it is even interpolated, as in "the idear of." French, as written and printed, is plastered all over with letters that are never sounded, though they waste much labor when they are written.

The waste of time in spelling imaginary sounds and their history (or etymology as it is called) is monstrous in English and French; and so much has been written on the subject that it is quite stale, because the writers have dwelt only on the anomalies of our orthography, which are merely funny, and on the botheration of children by them. Nothing has been said of the colossal waste of time and material, though this alone is gigantic enough to bring about a reform so costly, so unpopular, and requiring so much mental effort as the introduction of a new alphabet and a new orthography. It is true that once the magnitude of the commercial saving is grasped because it has never yet been stated in figures, perhaps because they are incalculable, perhaps because if they were fully calculated, the statisticians might be compelled to make the unit a billion or so, just as the astronomers have been compelled to make their unit of distance a lightyear.

In any case the waste does not come home to the layman. For example, take the two words tough and cough. He may not have to write them for years, if at all. Anyhow he now has tough and cough so thoroughly fixed in his head and everybody else's that he would be set down as illiterate if he wrote tuf and cof; consequently a reform would mean for him simply a lot of trouble not worth taking. Consequently the layman, always in a huge majority, will fight spelling reform tooth and nail. As he cannot be convinced, his opposition must be steam-rollered by the overworked writers and printers who feel the urgency of the reform.

Though I am an author, I also am left cold by tough and cough; for I, too, seldom write them. But take the words though and should and enough: containing eighteen letters. Heaven knows how many hundred thousands times I have had to write these constantly recurring words. With a new English alphabet replacing the old Semitic one with its added Latin vowels I should be able to spell t-h-o-u-g-h with two letters, s-h-o-u-l-d with three, and e-n-o-u-g-h with four: nine letters instead of eighteen: a saving of a hundred per cent of my time and my typist's time and the printer's time, to say nothing of the saving in paper and wear and tear of machinery. As I have said, I save my own time by shorthand; but as it all has to go into longhand before it can be printed, and I cannot use shorthand for my holograph epistles, shorthand is no remedy. I also have the personal grievance, shared by all my namesakes, of having to spell my own name with four letters instead of the two a Russian uses to spell it with his alphabet of 35 letters. All round me I hear the corruption of our language produced by the absurd device of spelling the first sound in my name with the two letters sh. London is surrounded by populous suburbs which began as homes or "hams" and grew to be hamlets or groups of hams. One of them is still called Peter's Ham, another Lewis Ham. But as these names are now spelt as one word this lack of a letter in our alphabet for the final sound in wish, and our very misleading use of sh to supply the deficiency, has set everyone calling them Peter Sham and Louis Sham. Further off, in Surrey, there is a place named Cars Halton. Now it is called Car Shallton. Horse Ham is called Hor-shm. Colt Hurst, which is good English, is called Coal Thirst, which is nonsense. For want of a letter to indicate the final sound in Smith we have Elt Ham and El Tham. We have no letter for the first and last consonant in church, and are given to the absurd expedient of representing it by ch. Someday we shall have Chichester called Chick Hester. A town formerly known as Sisseter is so insanely misspelt that it is now called Siren.

But the lack of consonants is a trifle beside our lack of vowels. The Latin alphabet gives us five, whereas the least we can write phonetically with is eighteen. I do not mean that there are only eighteen vowels in daily use: eighteen hundred would be nearer the truth. When I was chairman of the Spoken English Committee of the British Broadcasting Corporation it was easy enough to get a unanimous decision that exemplary and applicable should be pronounced with the stress on the first syllable, though the announcers keep on putting the stress on the second all the same; but when the announcers asked us how they should pronounce cross or launch there were as many different pronunciations of the vowels as there were members present. I secured a decision in favor of my own pronunciation of launch by the happy accident that it was adopted by King George the Fifth when christening a new liner on the Clyde. But the members were perfectly intelligible to one another in spite of their ringing all the possible changes between crawz and cross, between lanch and lawnch. To get such common words as son and science phonetically defined was hopeless. In what is called the Oxford accent son and sun became san; sawed and sword are pronounced alike; and my native city becomes Dablin. In Dublin itself I have heard it called Dawblin. The Oxford pronunciation of science is sahyence: the Irish pronunciation is sŭ-yence. Shakespear pronounced wind as wined; and as late as the end of the eighteenth century an attempt to correct an actor who pronounced it in this way provoked the retort "I cannot finned it in my minned to call it winned." Rosalind is on the stage ridiculously pronounced Rozzalinned though Shakespear called her Roh-za-lined, rhyming it to "If a cat will after kind." Kind, by the way, should logically be pronounced kinned. The word trist is again so far out of use that nobody knows how to pronounce it. It should rhyme to triced, but is mostly supposed to rhyme to kissed. The first vowel in Christ and Christendom has two widely different sounds, sometimes absurdly described as long i and short i; but both are spelt alike.

I could fill pages with instances; but my present point is not to make lists of anomalies, but to shew that (a) the English language cannot be spelt with five Latin vowels, and (b) that though the vowels used by English people are as various as their faces yet they understand one another's speech well enough for all practical purposes, just as whilst Smith's face differs from Jones's so much that the one could not possibly be mistaken for the other yet they are so alike that they are instantly recognizable as man and man, not as cat and dog. In the same way it is found that though the number of different vowel sounds we utter is practically infinite yet a vowel alphabet of eighteen letters can indicate a speech sufficiently unisonal to be understood generally, and to preserve the language from the continual change which goes on at present because the written word teaches nothing as to the pronunciation, and frequently belies it. Absurd pseudo-etymological spellings are taken to be phonetic, very soon in the case of words that are seldom heard, more slowly when constant usage keeps tradition alive, but none the less surely. When the masses learn to read tay becomes tee and obleezh becomes oblydge at the suggestion of the printed word in spite of usage. A workman who teaches himself to read pronounces semi- as see my. I myself, brought up to imitate the French pronunciation of envelope, am now trying to say enn-velope like everybody else.

Sometimes the change is an aesthetic improvement. My grandfather swore "be the varchoo" of his oath: I prefer vert-yoo. Edge-i-cate is less refined than ed-you-cate. The late Helen Taylor, John Stuart Mill's stepdaughter, who as a public speaker always said Russ-ya and Pruss-ya instead of Rusher and Prussher, left her hearers awestruck. The indefinite article, a neutral sound sometimes called the obscure vowel, and the commonest sound in our language though we cannot print it except by turning an e upside down, was always pronounced by Mrs. Annie Besant, perhaps the greatest British oratress of her time, as if it rhymed with pay. In short, we are all over the shop with our vowels because we cannot spell them with our alphabet. Like Scott, Dickens, Artemus Ward and other writers of dialect I have made desperate efforts to represent local and class dialects by the twenty-six letters of the Latin alphabet, but found it impossible and had to give it up. A well-known actor, when studying one of my cockney parts, had to copy it in ordinary spelling before he could learn it.

My concern here, however, is not with pronunciation but with the saving of time wasted. We try to extend our alphabet by writing two letters instead of three; but we make a mess of this device. With reckless inconsistency we write sweat and sweet, and then write whet and wheat, just the contrary. Consistency is not always a virtue; but spelling becomes a will o' the wisp without it. I have never had much difficulty in spelling, because as a child I read a good deal, and my unusual memory was good; but people who do not read much or at all, and whose word memory is aural, cannot spell academically, and are tempted to write illegibly to conceal this quite innocent inability, which they think disgraceful because illiteracy was for centuries a mark of class.

But neither speech nor writing can now be depended on as class indexes. Oxford graduates and costermongers alike call the sun the san and a rose a rah-ooze. The classical scholar and Poet Laureate John Dryden said yit and git where we say yet and get: another instance of spelling changing pronunciation instead of simply noting it. The Duke of Wellington dropped the h in humble and hospital, herb and hustler. So did I in my youth, though, as we were both Irish, h-dropping as practised in England and France was not native to us. I still say onner and our instead of honour and hour. Everybody does. Probably before long we shall all sing "Be it ever so umbl there's no place like ome," which is easier and prettier than "Be it evvah sah-oo hambl *etc.*"

I have dealt with vowels so far; but whenever an Englishman can get in an extra vowel and make it a diphthong he does so. When he tries to converse in French he cannot say *coupé* or *entrez:* he says coopay and ongtray. When he is in the chorus at a performance of one of the great Masses—say Bach's in B minor—he addresses the Almighty as Tay instead of making the Latin e a vowel. He calls gold gah-oold. Price, a very common word, is sometimes prah-ees, sometimes prawce, sometimes proyce, and sometimes, affectedly, prace. That is why our attempts to express our eighteen vowels with five letters by doubling them will not work: we cannot note down the diphthongal pronunciation until we have a separate single letter for every vowel, so that we can stop such mispronunciations as reel and ideel for real and ideal, and write diphthongs as such. The middle sound in beat, spelt with two letters, is a single pure vowel. The middle sound in bite, also spelt with two letters, is a diphthong. The spelling l-i-g-h-t is simply insane.

The worst vulgarism in English speech is a habit of prefixing the neutral vowel, which phoneticians usually indicate by e printed upside down, to all the vowels and diphthongs. The woman who asks for "e kapp e te-ee" is at once classed as, at best, lower middle. When I pass an elementary school and hear the children repeating the alphabet in unison, and chanting unrebuked "Ah-yee, Be-yee, Ce-yee, De-yee" I am restrained from going in and shooting the teacher only by the fact that I do not carry a gun and by my fear of the police. Not that I cannot understand the children when they speak; but their speech is ugly; and euphony is very important. By all means give us an adequate alphabet, and let people spell as they speak without any nonsense about bad or good or right or wrong spelling and speech; but let them remember that if they make ugly or slovenly sounds when they speak they will never be respected. This is so well known that masses of our population are bilingual. They have an official speech as part of their company manners which they do not use at home or in conversation with their equals. Sometimes they had better not. It is extremely irritating to a parent to be spoken to by a child in a superior manner; so wise children drop their school acquirements with their daddies and mummies. All such domestic friction would soon cease if it became impossible for us to learn to read and write without all learning to speak in the same way.

And now what, exactly, do I want done about it? I will be quite precise. I want our type designers, or artist-calligraphers, or whatever they call themselves, to design an alphabet capable of representing the sounds of the following string of nonsense quite unequivocally without using two letters to represent one sound or making the same letter represent different sounds by diacritical marks. The rule is to be One Sound One Letter, with every letter unmistakably different from all the others. Here is the string of nonsense. An alphabet which will spell it under these conditions will spell any English word well enough to begin with.

> Chang at leisure was superior to Lynch in his rouge, munching a lozenge at the burial in Merrion Square of Hyperion the Alien who valued his billiards so highly.
>
> Quick! quick! hear the queer story how father and son one time sat in the house man to man eating bread and telling the tale of the fir on the road to the city by the sea following the coast to its fall full two fathoms deep. There they lived together served by the carrier, whose narrower mind through beer was sore and whose poor boy shivered over the fire all day lingering in a tangle of tactless empty instinct ineptly swallowing quarts of stingo.

As well as I can count, this sample of English contains 372 sounds, and as spelt above requires 504 letters to print it, the loss in paper, ink, wear and tear of machinery, compositors' time, machinists' time, and author's time being over 26%, which could be saved by the use of the alphabet I ask for. I repeat that this figure, which means nothing to the mass of people who, when they write at all, seldom exceed one sheet of notepaper, is conclusive for reform in the case of people who are writing or typing or printing all day. Calligraphers intelligent enough to grasp its importance will, if they have read these pages, rush to their drawing boards to seize the opportunity.

The first question that will occur to them is how many letters they will have to design; for it will seem only commonsense to retain the 26 letters of the existing alphabet and invent only the ones in which it is deficient. But that can only serve if every letter in the 26 is given a fixed and invariable sound. The result would be a spelling which would not only lead the first generation of its readers to dismiss the writers as crudely illiterate, but would present unexpected obscenities which no decent person could be induced to write. The new alphabet must be so different from the old that no one could possibly mistake the new spelling for the old.

This disposes of all the attempts at "simplified spelling" with the old alphabet. There is nothing for it but to design 24 new consonants and 18 new vowels, making in all a new alphabet of 42 letters, and use it side by side with the present lettering until the better ousts the worse.

The artist-calligraphers will see at first only an opportunity for 42 beautiful line drawings to make a printed book as decorative as a panel by Giovanni da Udine, and a handwritten sonnet as delightful visually as one by Michael Angelo, the most perfect of all calligraphers. But that will never do. The first step is to settle the alphabet on purely utilitarian lines and then let the artists make it as handsome as they can.

For instance, a straight line, written with a single stroke of the pen, can represent four different consonants by varying its length and position. Put a hook at the top of it, and you have four more consonants. Put a hook at the lower end, and you have four more, and put hooks at both ends and you have another four; so that you have 16 consonants writable by one stroke of the pen. The late Henry Sweet, still our leading authority on British phonetics, begins his alphabet in this way, achieving at one stroke p, t, k, and ch; b, d, g (hard) and j; m, n, ng and the ni in companion; kw, r, Spanish double l and the r in superior. He takes our manuscript e and l (different lengths of the same sign) and gets f, s, and zh. Turning it backwards he gets v, z, and sh. He takes our c and o, and gets dh and th. A waved stroke gives him l; and thus, borrowing only four letters from our alphabet, he obtains the required 24 consonants, leaving 22 of our letters derelict. For vowels he resorts to long and short curves at two levels, with or without little circles attached before or after, and thus gets the requisite 18 new letters easily. Thus the utilitarian task of inventing new letters has already been done by a first rate authority. The artists have only to discover how to make the strokes and curves pleasing to the eye.

At this point, however, the guidance of Henry Sweet must be dropped; for when he had completed his alphabet he proceeded to bedevil it into an instrument for verbatim reporting, which is the art of jotting down, not all the sounds uttered by a public speaker, which is beyond manual dexterity, but enough of them to remind the practised reporter of the entire words. He writes zah and depends on his memory or on the context to determine whether this means exact or example or examine or exasperate or what not. After seven years' practice Sweet became so expert at this sort of guessing that the specimens he gives in his Manual of Current Shorthand (published by the Clarendon Press) are unreadable by anyone lacking the experience.

This is true of all reporting systems. There are dozens of them in existence; and they are all efficient enough; for the debates of Cromwell's Ironsides and the cross-examinations of St. Joan are on record. Charles Dickens was a competent verbatim reporter before any of the systems now in use were invented. Sweet's contractions and guessings were therefore quite superfluous: what was needed from him was an alphabet with which the English language could be unequivocally spelt at full length, and not a new reporting shorthand.

Now Sweet, being a very English Englishman, was extremely quarrelsome. Being moreover the brainiest Oxford don of his time, he was embittered by the contempt with which his subject, to say nothing of himself, was treated by his university, which was and still is full of the medieval notion, valid enough for King Richard Lionheart but madly out of date today, that English is no language for a gentleman, and is tolerable only as a means of communication with the lower classes. His wrath fell on his forerunner Isaac Pitman, whose shorthand he called the Pitfall system. Pitman had anticipated Sweet's strokes; but he made their interpretation depend on their thickness and the direction in which they were written. Thus a horizontal stroke meant k, and a vertical one t. The strokes slanting half-way between meant p and ch. The same strokes thickened gave him g, d, b, and j, with the addition of r for ch written upward instead of downward. Thus he got nine letters from the single stroke, and would have got ten if an upstroke could be thickened, which is not possible as a feat of penmanship. Sweet discarded these distinctions because, as no two people write at the same slant, the stroke should have only one meaning no matter at what slant it is written. Making strokes at different slants is drawing, not writing; and Sweet insisted that writing must be *currente calamo:* hence he called his script Current Shorthand. Thick and thin he discarded as unpractical for upstrokes and pencil work. His getting rid of these elaborations was an important improvement. The distinctions he substituted were those to which the old printed alphabet has accustomed us.

In it the stroke projects sometimes above the line of writing as in the letter l, sometimes below it as in the letter j, sometimes neither above nor below as in the letter i, sometimes both above and below as in our manuscript p, f and capital j. This gave Sweet only four letters per simple stroke instead of Pitman's nine; but four are more than enough. Also much of the pen work imposed by our alphabet is unnecessary: for instance, m and w take twice as long to write as l though they can be indicated quite as briefly; and p and q could be indicated by their projecting strokes alone without attaching an n to the p and an o to the q.

I take it then that the new English alphabet will be based on Sweet, and not on Pitman, though I am writing this preface in Pitman's shorthand and not in Sweet's, having discarded Sweet's reporting contractions as unnecessary for my purpose and puzzling for my transcriber. The designer of the new alphabet will find that Sweet has done all the preliminary study for him, and solved its utilitarian problems.

What remains to be done is to make the strokes and hooks and curves and circles look nice. If very young, the designer may ask me indignantly whether I think of the beauty sought by artists as something to be stuck on to the inventions of the pedant. In this case it is. An architect has to make a house beautiful; but the house, if it is to be lived in, must be dictated by the needs of its inhabitants and not by the architect's fancies. The great printers, Jensen, Caslon, Morris, did not invent letters: they made the old ones pleasing as well as legible, and made books worth looking at as well as reading. What they did for the old alphabet their successors must do for the new. There is plenty of scope for invention as well as for decoration: for instance, Sweet's alphabet has no capitals nor has Pitman's. Neither has any italics. Since Morris revived printing as a fine art, scores of new types have come into the market. Morris himself designed several.

The new alphabet, like the old, will not be written as printed: its calligraphers will have to provide us with a new handwriting. Our present one is so unwritable and illegible that I am bothered by official correspondents asking me to write my name "in block letters, please," though a good handwriting is more legible and far prettier than block, in which the letters, being the same height, cannot give every word a characteristic shape peculiar to itself. Shakespeare's signature, though orthographically illegible, is, when once you have learnt it, much more instantaneously recognizable and readable than SHAKESPEARE, which at a little distance might be CHAMBERLAIN or any other word of eleven letters.

Other changes and developments in the use of language and the art of writing may follow the introduction of an English alphabet. There is, for instance, the Basic English of the Orthological Institute at 10, King's Parade, Cambridge, by which foreigners can express all their wants in England by learning 800 English words. It is a thought-out pidgin, and gets rid of much of our grammatical superfluities. The Institute is, as far as I know, the best live organ for all the cognate reforms, as the literary Societies and Academies do nothing but award medals and read historical and critical lectures to one another.

The various schools of shorthand teach new alphabets; but they are wholly preoccupied with verbatim reporting, which is a separate affair. Their triumphs are reckoned in words per minute written at speeds at which no language can be fully written at all. They train correspondence clerks very efficiently; but they should pay more attention to authors and others whose business it is to write, and who cannot carry secretaries or dictaphones about with them everywhere. Such scribes can write at their own pace, and need no reporting contractions, which only waste their time and distract their attention, besides presenting insoluble puzzles to the typist who has to transcribe them. I have long since discarded them. On these terms shorthand is very easy to learn. On reporting terms it takes years of practice to acquire complete efficiency and then only in cases of exceptional natural aptitude, which varies curiously from individual to individual.

The only danger I can foresee in the establishment of an English alphabet is the danger of civil war. Our present spelling is incapable of indicating the sounds of our words and does not pretend to; but the new spelling would prescribe an official pronunciation. Nobody at present calls a lam a lamb or pronounces wawk and tawk as walk and talk. But when the pronunciation can be and is indicated, the disputable points will be small enough for the stupidest person to understand and fight about. And the ferocity with which people fight about words is astonishing. In London there is a street labelled Conduit Street. When the word conduit, like the thing, went out of use, cabmen were told to drive to Cundit Street. They are still so told by elderly gentlemen. When modern electric engineering brought the word into common use the engineers called it con-dew-it. A savage controversy in the columns of The Times ensued. I tried to restore good humor by asking whether, if the London University decided to pay a compliment to our Oriental dominions by calling one of its new streets Pundit Street it would be spelt Ponduit Street. I had better have said nothing; for I was instantly assailed as a profane wretch trifling with a sacred subject. Englishmen may yet kill one another and bomb their cities into ruin to decide whether v-a-s-e spells vawz or vahz or vaiz. Cawtholic or Kahtholic may convulse

Ireland when the national question is dead and buried. We shall all agree that h-e-i-g-h-t is an orthographic monstrosity; but when it is abolished and we have to decide whether the official pronunciation shall be hite or hyth, there will probably be a sanguinary class war; for in this case the proletarian custom is more logical than the Oxford one.

Still, we must take that risk. If the introduction of an English alphabet for the English language costs a civil war, or even, as the introduction of summer time did, a world war, I shall not grudge it. The waste of war is negligible in comparison to the daily waste of trying to communicate with one another in English through an alphabet with sixteen letters missing. That must be remedied, come what may.

Ayot St. Lawrence

"SPELLING REFORM: EXTRACT FROM THE OFFICIAL REPORT"

Excerpts from Debate on the SPELLING REFORM BILL in the House of Commons, Friday, 11th March, 1949

The progress of *spelling* reform in English has been deeply affected by Shaw's ideas and writings on *alphabet* reform. For example, GBS' statements were quoted and hence played a role in the debate on the Spelling Reform Bill in Commons, though Shaw did not participate directly, and did not even support the bill under discussion.

The Spelling Reform Bill was introduced by Mr. Mont Follick, Member from Loughborough—like Shaw, an intellectual maverick. Follick had previously introduced a bill on the same subject in 1945. In introducing the 1949 legislation, Follick rejected the advice of more circumspect leaders of the Simplified Spelling Society of Great Britain. They had urged avoidance of attempts at legislation that suggested governmental intervention or compulsion.

During the debate, Mr. I. J. (now Sir James) Pitman, a veteran Simplified Spelling Society supporter, became Follick's active collaborator. While the Spelling Reform Bill lost by the narrow margin of 87 noes to 84 ayes, the debate gave reform of English spelling "a good standing advertisement." Perhaps, as Mr. Tomlinson, the Minister of Education, contended in his remarks in opposition to the Bill, the bill was lost because "the promoters of the Bill have tried to prove too much in too short a time." The "Simplified Spelling Bill," debated on February 27, 1953, met with better success on an early reading, 65 ayes to 53 noes. It was withdrawn by its proponents with the understanding that the Minister of Education would support research in the use of simplified spelling for improved reading, a promise which is now being kept.

True to British parliamentary tradition, the debate was illuminated by flashes of keen wit. Sir A. P. Herbert, representing Oxford University, raised the question of how the new spelling, which purported to reflect pronunciation phonetically, would deal with the word "water." Would it be spelled as pronounced by Cockneys, "wa-er"? or as spoken by Americans, "iced wotter?"

"But how do the Scotsmen say it? Is there a Scotsman in the House who can tell us?" he asked.

The answer came swiftly from Mr. Rankin of Glasgow: "We pronounce it 'whisky.'"

At another point in the debate, Mr. Follick quoted the venerable Lloyd George as having said, "If we could only have in English the rational alphabet we have in Welsh, English would become the world language over-night." Nevertheless, Follick added that Lloyd George's son, an M.P., had not yet made up his mind about the bill. A colleague solemnly pronounced ironical judgment: "He is a Liberal."

To the claims in Follick's heady rhetoric that adoption of the Spelling Reform Bill would promote peace because it would help English to become the universal language, Mr. Hollis gently admonished; "History gives no reason to think that we would cease fighting one another merely because we talked the same language. I do not think we would like Mr. Molotov any better if we understood everything that he said."

America, too, has had a vigorous and active history of attempts at spelling reform, although it is currently dormant. The inactive movement has recently shown signs of revitalization in the intensive interest over the use of simpler spelling to improve reading instruction. A bill to promote spelling reform, somewhat in imitation of the British model, was introduced into the U.S.

Congress in March, 1957 by Representative Harlan Hagen of California.

Support for a spelling reform movement has had long precedent in the American tradition. Among its proponents have been men and organizations of considerable influence: Benjamin Franklin, Noah Webster, Melvil Dewey, Francis A. March, William T. Harris, Brander Matthews, Theodore Roosevelt, Mark Twain; the American Philological, Spelling Reform, and National Education Associations, the Simplified Spelling Board, and most recently, the Simpler Spelling Association. At various times, there have been Congressional debates and resolutions, newspaper editorials and cartoons, conferences and all the other paraphernalia and appurtenances of a full-blown crusade. The outstanding contemporary American proponent is Dr. Godfrey Dewey, Secretary of the Simpler Spelling Association, Lake Placid, New York, whose work was referred to in the Commons' Debate.

These excerpts from the Commons' Debate of 1949 include references to Shaw and his work.

HOUSE OF COMMONS

[*Extract from the Official Report*]

SPELLING REFORM

(March 11, 1949)

Mr. Follick (*Loughborough*): Those are my interests, and before proceeding with my speech I ought from this place to thank one or two people who have helped me considerably and encouraged me not to lose hope but to go ahead with this project. First in the line comes that great literary genius, philosopher and cantankerous recluse, Bernard Shaw. In his own peculiar way he helps people. He is untiring in his help and he has helped me more than I can possibly say.

Mr. I. J. Pitman (Bath): We are not pressing for a particular system or compulsion but for the general principle. Mr. Bernard Shaw has often said that the two will run concurrently and that the best will eventually supersede the present system. All he wants is a 40-letter alphabet. To my certain knowledge he has offered the whole of his estate to the Minister of Education for the financing of just the sort of thing about which I have been speaking, provided that it is in the 40-letter alphabet.

The House might be interested in this letter sent to me this week by Mr. Bernard Shaw:

"The Bill as it stands with its compulsory and exclusive items is impossible; but it can be made practicable in Committee; and its defeat would be an international calamity. Nevertheless the House will be frightened off as it always has been by the cost of replacing scrapped printers' plant and typewriters, rearranging and reprinting dictionaries and encyclopedias, transmogrifying the Bible and all the masterpieces of our literature. It has never taken into account the hard fact that a British alphabet of 40 letters would make it possible by rational spelling to save 20 per cent. *per minute* in time and labor, and that 20 per cent. per minute is more than half a million per cent. per year. If that figure does not make Sir Stafford Cripps as keen on spelling reform as Mr. Follick nothing will.

"But a beginning can be made with existing plant.

The addition of 14 letters to the present alphabet can be obtained provisionally by handsetting with 14 of the letters turned upside down or with borrowings from the Greek alphabet which all considerable printers stock. By this device school primers can be rationally spelt and children enabled to spell as they pronounce and have their mispronunciations corrected by their teacher.

"Although I did not begin writing plays until I was 40, I have written 17 more plays than Shakespeare did besides bulky political treatises bringing Socialism up to date, and a mass of critical essays in Art and Science, to say nothing of letters to 'The Times.' Such an output would have been utterly impossible had it not been drafted in Pitman's 40 letter phonographic alphabet. Keep your eye on your father Isaac;"——

I think he really means my grandfather—

"and he will pull you through. But perhaps you had better not mention this in Debate as hon. Members may not be quite unanimous in regarding my activities as a boon and a blessing."

Why is it that Mr. Bernard Shaw can reasonably say that the defeat of the Bill today would be an international calamity? The answer is that the benefits of the Bill will be a colossal contribution to humanity, possibly as great as that made by the invention of printing. Let us look at the matter from two points of view, that of the British people and that of other peoples in the world, dividing these latter into the English-speaking and the speakers of other languages. In the English-speaking category of the other people of the world we must consider that great republic the United States of

America. Do not let any hon. Member feel that there is any danger on technical grounds of our failing to carry the two nations together.

I have here a letter which I received this morning, written by Dr. Godfrey Dewey, chairman of the Simpler Spelling Committee, Lake Placid Club Education Foundation, and Secretary of the Simpler Spelling Association. He says:

"I speak, therefore, for the organised spelling reform movement in this country, in assuring you of our hearty support of your present efforts."

He goes on to say:

"A committee such as that proposed by your Bill should be able to work out a scheme of rational spelling acceptable to both countries, with incalculable benefit to all English-speaking people, and indeed to the whole world."

Mr. Hollis: The hon. Member for Loughborough, with characteristic courtesy, has sent me a copy of the correspondence which has passed between the hon. Member and Mr. Bernard Shaw, but I cannot see how that correspondence in any way strengthens his case, because it was obvious that each of these distinguished people who thought that a scheme of simplified spelling would be a good idea each thought that the other's scheme would make spelling a great deal more complicated. For the moment, the hon. Member for Loughborough wants a scheme of simplified spelling which will take less time to learn, for which there is something to be said. Mr. Bernard Shaw wants a scheme which will take less time to write, for which there is also something to be said. But the two principles are entirely different principles. These ideas would produce two quite different schemes of spelling reform.

Mr. Pitman: Would my hon. Friend allow me? Mr. Shaw's system is both easier to learn and quicker to write.

Mr. Hollis: My hon. Friend now poses as arbitrator between the claims of the hon. Member for Loughborough and those of Bernard Shaw. The hon. Member for Loughborough does not agree that what Mr. Shaw wants is simpler, and Mr. Shaw does not agree that what the hon. Member for Loughborough wants is simpler, and who am I to arbitrate between the two? Mr. Bernard Shaw makes a calculation of the time wasted by people putting a "b" at the end of the word "bomb," but, if we had not spent time in putting a "b" at the end of the word "bomb," just think how many worse things we might have been doing. But that second "b" is not wholly purposeless because the second "b" at the end of the word makes it easier for the learner to learn the relationship between "bomb" and, say, "bombardment" or "bombardier." Yet I see a certain amount of common sense in the maxim that we should try to spell as we pronounce, but the difficulty is that people pronounce English entirely differently from one another, and the reason why they understand it is only because they all spell it the same.

Mr. Tomlinson: We have heard a great deal today about Mr. George Bernard Shaw's unwearied championship of the idea of a rationalised spelling. Not all Mr. Shaw's ideas have proved acceptable to the people of this country, but that does not mean necessarily that they are not good ideas. I should be the last person to suggest that in the realm of language and literature his opinion is one that should be lightly disregarded. In recounting Mr. George Bernard Shaw's argument for the reform of our spelling, some of my hon. Friends have not given due consideration to his views on the question of legislation. Perhaps the House will allow me to quote from a letter which Mr. George Bernard Shaw wrote to my Department four or five years ago. He was discussing a scheme:

"to defray the cost of designing and introducing a British alphabet, transliterating the masterpieces of English literature and our school reading books into it and publishing the transliterations, advertising these publications and propagating their desirability, and, always without tampering with the existing alphabet, launching the other in competition with it until one of the two proves the fitter to survive. Official adoption or compulsion must wait upon prevalence; any attempt to begin with them would prove the political inexperience and incompetence of their advocates."

That is Mr. George Bernard Shaw, not me. What he says about legislation in this direction is a far better way of explaining it than I could. He points out that any attempt to begin would prove the inexperience of those who sought to apply it.

Mr. Pitman: Our proposal is what Bernard Shaw in that letter has submitted to the Minister.

Mr. Tomlinson: I would, however, commend especially to the House the last point of Mr. Shaw that "official adoption or compulsion must wait upon prevalence." There in a nutshell, expressed with his inimitable brevity and logic, is the main reason why the Government do not favour legislation on the lines of the Bill we are discussing. A little later on Mr. Shaw underlines this point when he says the adoption of a rationalised spelling

"for official publications and national records, and its tuition in public schools; in short, its virtual enforcement for general use, will not occur until its utility enforces itself. Meanwhile, the existing generation must have its literature in the form to which it is accustomed, reading and spelling by visual memory, not by ear."

That is George Bernard Shaw—by the way, I object to Mr. Shaw's objecting to the use of the Christian name "George," and I insist upon calling him George Bernard Shaw. He adds:

"I should strenuously object to have to read, much less write, my own works in a strange script, though I know I should get accustomed to it in a few weeks if I took that trouble."

"WESTMINSTER PHONETICS: SPELLING REFORM AS A TIME SAVER"

Letter to *The Times* of London (March 19, 1949)

Eight days after the Spelling Reform Debate in the House of Commons, GBS—a leading contender in absentia—had his say. He visited a plague on both houses. Shaw condemned "conventional Johnsonese orthography." With the expletive, "poppycock," he disposed of "Rational Spelling" as being worthy only of being "swept away, economically, because phonetic spelling with the present alphabet is impossible without the enormous expense of using two letters for one sound, and psychologically because without some new letters simplified spelling looks illiterate or childish."

GBS pointed out the anachronistic confusion that equated the original "Shakespear" or the King James Bible with the text in its present spelling, because we have become familiar with the orthography in the "outrageous transmogrification" of "Johnsonese." Shaw thus stigmatized the popularly accepted orthography based on the work of lexicographer Samuel Johnson and his *A Dictionary of the English Language* of 1755. Those spellings became the accepted style of printers, universities, dictionaries and the public, despite many curious linguistic and etymological errors, and many phonetic inconsistencies. "Johnsonese" is, of course, our conventional spelling, modified by some few changes introduced into American orthography under the influence of

Noah Webster in the early nineteenth century, and by the work of the Simplified Spelling Board of the twentieth.

Shaw contended that "what we immediately need is not an international language, nor an official persecution of Johnsonese, nor a New Spelling Bible or Old Spelling Shakespear, nor an alphabet of more than 40 letters, nor a revival of Bell's Visible Speech, nor any of the scores of phonetic fads that now confuse the issue and defeat reform, but a statistical enquiry into the waste of labor by Johnsonese spelling." The phrase "statistical enquiry" was a key one in Shaw's Will, made the next year.

WESTMINSTER PHONETICS
SPELLING REFORM AS A TIME-SAVER

(March, 19, 1949)

TO THE EDITOR OF THE TIMES

Sir,—Mr. Follick and Mr. Pitman have been lucky enough to break virtually even with a pitiably recalcitrant Cabinet over spelling reform.

In the debate Sir Alan Herbert took the field as the representative of Oxford University, the university of Henry Sweet, greatest of British phoneticians. After debiting the stale tomfooleries customary when spelling reform is discussed by novices and amateurs he finally extinguished himself by pointing out that a sample of Mr. Follick's spelling saves only one letter from the conventional Johnsonese orthography. This was the champion howler of the debate. I invite Sir Alan to write down that one letter, and measure how long it takes him to get it on paper, and how much paper it covers: say a fraction of a second and of a square inch. "Not worth saving" is his present *reductio ad absurdum.* But surely a University Member must be mathematician enough to go deeper. In the English-speaking world, on which the sun never sets, there are at every fraction of a moment millions of scribes, from bookkeepers to poets, writing that letter or some other single letter. If it is superfluous, thousands of acres of paper, months of time, and the labor of armies of men and women are being wasted on it. Dare Sir Alan now repeat that a difference of one letter does not matter?

The rest is poppycock. Simplified spelling, Rational spelling, Symphonic spelling, are swept away, economically because phonetic spelling with the present alphabet is impossible without the enormous expense of using two letters for one sound, and psychologically because without some new letters simplified spelling looks illiterate or childish. The notion that the value of the Bible and the plays of Shakespear lies in their spelling, and will vanish if it be changed, need not trouble anyone primitive enough to entertain it, seeing that both have survived the outrageous transmogrification of changing their spelling to Johnsonese. The fact that no two people have the same vowels any more than the same fingerprints does not matter provided they understand one another's speech. Oxford graduates, inhabitants of the Isle of Dogs, and most costermongers, will still call my native country Awlint, and speak, not as I do of sun and luggage but of san and laggij. No matter: we understand.

In short, what we immediately need is not an international language, nor an official persecution of Johnsonese, nor a New Spelling Bible or Old Spelling Shakespear, nor an alphabet of more than 40 letters, nor a revival of Bell's Visible Speech, nor any of the scores of phonetic fads that now confuse the issue and defeat reform, but a statistical enquiry into the waste of labor by Johnsonese spelling. The rest may be left to the Minister of Education, be he Labor, Conservative, Liberal, Communist, or what not. The roughest estimate will be irresistible; and until it is made public the promotion of Spelling Reform Bills by private members will be waste of time.

G. Bernard Shaw

"THE PROBLEM OF A COMMON LANGUAGE"

a letter to *The Listener* (December 1, 1949)
reprinted in *The Atlantic Monthly* (November, 1950)

Shaw wrote a letter to *The Listener* on December 1, 1949, commenting on the B.B.C. lecture of Mr. Robert Birley, Headmaster of Eton. (This triggered off the correspondence with Reto Rossetti on the subject of Esperanto, reproduced in the next section.)

Thrifty Shaw, not one to overlook the economics of his labors, sent *The Atlantic Monthly* his letter to *The Listener*. It appeared in the *Atlantic* posthumously, as it turned out, in November, 1950, as an article titled, the same as the original, "The Problem of a Common Language." Unfortunately, *The Atlantic* reproduced exactly a typographical error in the original, transliterating the word "shell" into "shall" in the third sentence of the second paragraph, thus completely vitiating the meaning of that sentence.

The dominant themes of Shaw's earlier writings were repeated: the colossal waste and cost of "Johnsonese" spelling; the consequent inability of children to write or speak English well, after years of instruction; the absurdity of attempts at international language adoption, especially of the artificial genre; the absolute economic folly of refusing to spell English phonetically so as to save enormous sums of money; and the promotion of Pidgin English as the perfect lingua franca—sans prolixity, sans inflections, sans grammar, but especially, sans Johnsonese irrational spelling.

The waste in time and money is the chief enemy—not the difficulties of children in learning to read. Shaw's final efforts in language reform were related to the larger motives of his ideas—a "life more abundant."

The *Atlantic* introduced the article in this way:

Britain's most distinguished dramatist, whose plays, letters, and postcards have delighted people the world over, George Bernard Shaw *is just a little wiser and older than the* Atlantic, *and continues to be one of its liveliest contributors. He was born in Dublin in July, 1856; captured London twenty years later; in 1884 he became the leading spirit of the Fabian Society; and in 1925 he received the Nobel Prize for Literature.*

THE PROBLEM OF A COMMON LANGUAGE

by G. BERNARD SHAW

(*Atlantic Monthly,* November, 1950)

Mr. Robert Birley, in his third Reith broadcast, culminating in a call for an international language and selecting French as the most probable choice (Spanish used to be the favorite), has gone very faithfully and competently over all the ground that has been surveyed again and again for a hundred years past without making any effective impression on either the public or the education authorities. It was all said by Alexander J. Ellis in his century-old book. I am old enough to have heard him lecture, in his velvet skull cap, for which he always apologised. After pleading his phonetic brief he read Shakespear's pronunciation just as Mr. Coghill now reads Chaucer. Since Ellis, we have had Pitman and Sweet, Volapuk and Esperanto, and no end of phonetic alphabets and shorthand systems; but we are still entangled in Johnson's absurd etymological bad spelling, wasting years of our lives in writing the single sounds of our language with two, three, four, five letters or more, and turning our children out of our elementary schools after nine years' daily instruction unable to speak or write English well enough to qualify them for clerical or professional appointments. All our phonetic propaganda is sterilised by the dread that the cost of the change would be colossal.

As a matter of fact, it is the cost of Johnsonese that is colossal: so colossal that it is beyond the comprehension of our authorities. Mr. Birley may argue until Doomsday for an international language, and plump for French as the best; but no authority will pay any serious attention until he puts the case into figures, and concentrates on labor saving as the only consideration that will cut any ice. The choice between French and English may turn on the fact that in French the very common word *shell* is spelt with eight letters and in English with five, of which one is superfluous. To appreciate this difference we must begin with the cost in time and labor of writing one alphabetic letter.

Take the word *debt.* Spell it det; and write it over and over again for a minute. Then do the same spelling it debt. The difference between the number of times you have written det and debt gives you the difference in time and labor between writing one letter of the alphabet and two.

If, like some of our spelling reformers and phoneticians, you are mathematically silly enough to play the old trick of disguising this difference as a percentage, you will get a figure too small to impress anybody. A percentage may mean a half-penny or a million pounds sterling, a fraction of a second or a thousand eons, a parish council or a world federation. Keep to the facts.

The first fact is that the difference you have counted is a difference per minute. It will prove to be 12 seconds. Therefore, as there are 365 days in the year, the difference is 73 days per individual scribe per year.

How many scribes are there? As the English language goes round the earth, the sun never setting on it, it is impossible to ascertain exactly how many people are writing it, not for one minute as an experiment, but all the time incessantly and perpetually. No matter: a big cross section will be just as conclusive. In the British Commonwealth and the United States of North America there are more than 270,000,000 born writers and speakers of English. Of these the proportion of authors, journalists, clerks, accountants, scholars, private correspondents and others writing continually and simultaneously all round the clock may safely be taken as one in every hundred, making 2,700,000. Multiply this figure by the 73 days. The answer is that every year in the cross section alone we are wasting 540,000 years of time and labor which we could save by spelling English phonetically enough for all practical purposes, adding to the Johnsonese alphabet fourteen letters, all of which can be borrowed provisionally from the stocks now held by our printers for setting up foreign and classical grammars, algebras, and the like.

I have left India, Pakistan, and Ceylon out of the calculation with their 400,000,000, whose dozen dialects are giving way to English. They would make the figures too enormous to be credible. One could only laugh. Enough to note that there is no industrial company on earth that would not scrap and replace all its plant, at whatever cost, to save in cost of production a fraction of such magnitudes. In the face of them it is folly to prattle vainly for the thousandth time about universal languages, teaching children to read, standard pronunciation, and the rest of the argy-bargy our phoneticians keep regurgitating.

It is Johnsonese that we cannot afford, not a forty-letter alphabet. For more than seventy years I have written books, plays, articles, and private letters, in legible phonetics, and thereby added at least two months every year to my productive lifetime as compared to Shakespear and Dickens, who had to write their works in longhand, though Dickens was an adept in reporting shorthand, which is unreadable by printers and typists.

I do not pretend to know what language will become international, though I agree with Mr. Birley that it will not be an artificial one. The fittest will survive. My guess is Pidgin English, the *lingua franca* of the Chinese coolie, the Australian black boy, and the traders and seafarers who employ them. It gets rid of the incubus of much useless grammar. In commercial Johnsonese we write "I regret to have to inform you that it is not possible for me to entertain the proposal in your esteemed letter." In Pidgin this is "Sorry no can." Pidgin, spoken or phonetically spelt, is a labor saving device which leaves the harvester, the internal combustion engine, and the telephone nowhere.

The case of children learning to read is an over-worked bugbear. Children learn to read and write by sight, not by sound. Those who have deficient visual memory spell phonetically and sign with a mark. Blind children read by touch, deaf ones lip read. I cannot remember any time when a page of print was unintelligible to me; so I can hardly have suffered much when learning.

Children should be taught to spell phonetically, and corrected only when their spelling betrays a mispronunciation, which for the present may be taken to mean a departure from the usage of Mr. Hibberd, chief announcer to the British Broadcasting Corporation. His vowels are much more representative and agreeable than those common to the University of Oxford and the Isle of Dogs.

A cockney who pronounces French in the accent of Stratford-atte-Bowe is actually more intelligible in France than the phonetic virtuoso who pronounces all but perfectly, barely a hundredth of every vowel being off the mark. The foreigner whose schooltaught English is excellent the day he arrives here speaks broken English after a year's residence, finding it quite sufficient for his purpose and an innocent amusement for his neighbors. All teachers should bear in mind that better is the enemy of good enough, and perfection not possible on any terms. Language need not and should not be taught beyond the point at which the speaker is understood. Not five minutes should be wasted in teaching a chauffeur who says "Them hills is very deceiving" to say "These mountain gorges are very deceptive." An English child who says "I thinked" or "I buyed" is just as intelligible as an adult who says "I thought" or "I bought."

We say that Time is Money. It is civilization, art, literature, leisure, pleasure: in short, life more abundant.

A LETTER AND POSTCARDS DEALING WITH AUXILIARY AND INTERNATIONAL LANGUAGES

(December, 1949 to January, 1950)
printed in "G.B. Shaw and Esperanto" in
The British Esperantist (July-August, 1960)

GBS carried on a prolific correspondence with people who wrote to him on various matters, including his language interests and ideas. (Shaw's letters are being edited, in many volumes, for publication in an authorized edition, by Professor Dan H. Laurence of New York University.) On the subject of alphabet and spelling reform, Shaw's chief British correspondence included Sir James Pitman, Miss Barbara Smoker of the Shaw Society, and Russell Scott, founder of the Phonetic Alphabet Association.

The Sage of Ayot St. Lawrence also numbered at least one American among his correspondents on these subjects, Samuel C. Seegay of New York City, an alphabet and spelling reform enthusiast. Ironically, GBS wrote in a letter to Sir James Pitman on September 16, 1944 that he had "never heard of Dewey" (Godfrey), to whom Pitman had referred as the foremost American advocate of spelling reform.

Russell Scott sent Shaw reports on developments in Sprechspur or "speech tracing," a symbol alphabet used experimentally in West Germany to teach children to read, and presumed to be equally applicable to English. Shaw wrote to Scott on January 12, 1950 disclaiming interest in the subject, because he wanted to have nothing to do with "teaching children to read." Furthermore, said GBS, he had no sympathy with any "universal language lunacy."

In a letter to Sir James Pitman on May 17, 1950, Shaw pointed out—as he had many times before—that no progress had been made by the international languages: Volapuk, Ido, Novial, or Esperanto. In his judgment, energy spent on this was a waste of time, like trying to convince the educational authorities, on whom no effect at all could be made.

In "Shaw and the Alphabet," in *The New Statesman and Nation* of January 26, 1957, Barbara Smoker quoted from a letter written by Shaw in 1950, only a few weeks before his death, to Russell Scott, who was still trying to interest Shaw in the phonetic script, Sprechspur, for economical printing and teaching of languages. Shaw said: "*Never waste time writing to very old men. I am 94, finished, I can do no more. You must carry on from where I left off.*" Though Mr. Scott, too, has died, Miss Smoker still crusades for the same goals through the Phonetic Alphabet Association of Great Britain.

In a letter to *The Listener* of December 1, 1949, Shaw advocated a form of pidgin English for international use. GBS was commenting on the broadcast lecture of Mr. Robert Birley, Headmaster of Eton, who had said, among other things, that "artificial languages" were unimportant since they "had no literature." On December 4, 1949, Reto Rossetti, a British educator and Esperantist, sent Shaw a copy of an open letter to Birley.

Writing to Shaw, Rossetti said, "You ought to be interested in my open letter to Mr. Birley, which I enclose. *The Listener* will not publish it, thus leaving the public with nothing to go by on the question of a common language but Birley's prejudiced ignorance and your amusing naivetes." Rossetti referred in this last remark to Shaw's letter in *The Listener* of December 1. Shaw replied on the 6th of December with one of his famous printed postcards, to which he had added in his own hand:

"Esperanto is not unique. There were many before it and have been many since. It is too inflected to have a chance of survival. You are evidently an innocent novice."

Rossetti replied, pointing out what he considered the fallacies in this statement, and distinguishing between "inflected" languages, like English, and an "agglutinated" one, like Esperanto, praising the virtues of the latter.

In a handwritten postcard reply, Shaw said:

"I heard all this about Volapuk nearly 70 years ago. Where is it now? My own favorite was Novial; but its inventor Jesperson chucked it.

"The inflections I mentioned are the grammatical ones. Norwegian and English inflections can give Zamenhof's native inflections the go-by (or kybosh) on that point.

"But what is the use of argybarging for the thousandth time about philology when the labor-saving possibilities are so overwhelming? Sweet and Lecky set me on to phonetics more than half a century ago: I was through the mill before you were born, and have come out with the conviction that the gate to reform is the economic one. I was the first to moot it; and the old stuff no longer interests me. Toothpicks like universal languages cannot move the world. So good luck to you; but damn your Esperanto! G.B.S."

In his reply, Rossetti protested Shaw's *ex cathedra* and sweeping condemnation of Esperanto, based on allegedly insufficient study, and concluded: "Thanks for your good luck wish. Very good luck to you too, sir, and I won't add 'damn your *phonetic English*', for I think it's a good thing. My own favourite language, you see, is a *phonetic one*."

Shaw replied on December 20 in a typewritten letter:

"Dear Mr. Rossetti,

Past experience suggests that Esperanto, now as prosperous

as Volapuk was, will in a few years be where Volapuk now is. But in the meantime your command of Esperanto is a very useful accomplishment, like the Morse, the A.B.C. or any other interlingual code. If it becomes a universal language through its survival as the fittest, let it. We shall see. I dislike its looks, as Chesterton did when he said that he could not bring himself to say 'Tearoj idle Tearoj. I know not what you mean.' This, of course, is nonsense but it explains my aesthetic preference for Novial. There is nothing in all this for us to disagree about.

"But why do you make your propaganda ridiculous by denouncing the views of a nonagenarian as naivetes. Beware of celebrities. I am a celebrity. Do not forget the famous retort of Ferdinand Lassalle. 'You are at a disadvantage, because if you call me a fool you will be certified as a lunatic, whereas if I call you a fool all Europe will believe me.' I may be a dotard but I was not naive in my prime; and I have been on this phonetic job for 70 years. Be as disrespectful as you like; but do not be absurd and quarrelsome.

"On no account must our correspondence be published. Everybody who gets a postcard from me wants to rush it into print. Our correspondence has been private, and must remain so.

G. Bernard Shaw."

Rossetti replied at once, apologizing for his phrase "amusing naivetes" and pointing out the vital difference between Volapuk and Esperanto, namely, that Zamenhof gave Esperanto freedom to evolve.

Three months later, Rossetti wrote to Shaw again, seeking permission to include a translation of *Back to Methuselah,* Part I, Act I, in the *Angla Antologio,* an Esperanto anthology.

Shaw's return postcard said:

"My contracts with my publishers, present and possible in the future, do not admit of competing Esperanto editions.

In any case I will not sanction excerpts; it must be the entire work or nothing. The question whether Esperanto is a foreign language, or legally any language at all, is one for which I have neither time or taste. Cut me out of your plans; I will not discuss them further. G.B.S."

From

Bernard Shaw

Phone & Wire: CODICOTE 218. AYOT SAINT LAWRENCE, WELWYN, HERTS.

23/3/1950

My contracts with my publishers, present and possible in the future, do not admit of competing Esperanto editions. In any case I will not sanction excerpts: it must be the entire work or nothing. The question whether Esp. is a foreign language, or legally any language at all, is one for which I have neither time nor taste. Cut me out of your plans: I will not discuss them further.

G.B.S.

Reproduction of hand-written post card to Dr. Reto Rossetti

4, Whitehall Court (116) London, S.W.1.
Telegrams : Socialist, Parl-London.
Telephone : Whitehall 3160.

Ayot Saint Lawrence, Welwyn, Herts.
Station : Welwyn Garden City, 5 miles.
Telegrams and Phone : Codicote 218.

11/12/1949

From

Bernard Shaw

I heard all this about Volapük nearly 70 years ago. Where is it now? My own favorite was Novial; but its inventor Jesperson himself chucked it.

The inflections I mentioned are the grammatical ones. Norwegian and English can give Zamenhof's native inflections the go-by (or kybosh) on that point.

But what is the use of argybarging for the thousandth time about philology when the labor saving possibilities are so overwhelming? Sweet and Lecky set me on to phonetics more than half a century ago: I was through the mill before you were born, and have come out with the conviction that the gate to reform is the economic one - I was the first to moot it; and the old stuff no longer interests me. Toothpicks like universal languages cannot move the world. So good luck to you; but damn your Esperanto! G.B.S.

Reproduction of hand-written post card to Dr. Reto Rossetti

From

Bernard Shaw

A FORTY LETTER BRITISH ALFABET

The number of letters in our Johnsonese alfabet, minus *x*, *c*, and *q* (unnecessary) is	23
The following consonants are missing : *sh*, *zh*, *wh*, *ch*, *th*, *dh*, and *ng* . .	7
Also missing are the vowels and dipthongs *ah*, *aw*, *at*, *et*, *it*, *ot*, *ut*, *oot*, *yoot*, and the neutral second vowel in *colour*, *labour*, *honor*, &c.	10
	40

A quite phonetic British alfabet is impossible because the vowels of British speakers differ as their finger prints do ; but the 40 sounds listed above will make them as intelligible to one another in writing as they now are in speech. Thus, though Oxford graduates and London costermongers pronounce son and sun as *san* and Ireland as *Awlnd*, they understand one another in conversation.

In Johnsonese the missing letters are indicated by using two or three letters for a single sound. For instance, *though* has six letters for two sounds. A 40 letter alfabet providing one unambiguous symbol for each sound would save manual labor at the rate of 25 per cent. per minute (131,400 per annum). Multiply this figure by the millions at every moment busy writing English somewhere in the world, and the total saving is so prodigious that the utmost cost of a change is negligible.

Children, who now have to master the multiplication and pence tables, could learn a 40 letter alfabet easily. Johnsonese is so full of inconsistencies that the few who can spell it do so not by the sound of the word but by the look of it.

6/12/1949 Esperanto is not unique. There were many before it and have been many since. It is too inflected to have a chance of survival. You are evidently an innocent novice.

Ayot Saint Lawrence,
Welwyn, Herts.

One of Shaw's famous post cards, bearing hand-written message.

EXCERPTS FROM "BERNARD SHAW'S WILL" (1950)

As early as 1944, Shaw had publicly indicated his intentions to include in his Will financial provisions to encourage the design and introduction of a new British alphabet. On July 19, 1944, he wrote to his friend, I.J. (now Sir James) Pitman that he intended to have his "residuary estate accumulate for 20 years" and "be available meanwhile for financing certain exactly defined and limited operations: to wit (a) designing a new British one-sound-one-letter alphabet, (b) the transliteration and depositing of copies in leading public libraries throughout the Commonwealth and elsewhere." GBS concluded the letter with the salutation that he proposed to "leave the field open to you to do the job with a grant in aid from the Public Trustee if you care to. You are, I should say, the best equipped adventurer in the field."

Shaw's Will was dated June 12, 1950. He died on November 2, 1950. The provisions of the Will were announced early in 1951.

The Public Trustee was made sole executor and trustee. Of the forty-seven clauses in the Will, those numbered 35, 36, 37, 38, 39 and 40 related to the matter of the "alphabet trust." They provided that the income of the residuary estate for twenty-one years was to be used by the Public Trustee to choose a Proposed British Alphabet of at least forty letters; to launch "statistical inquiries" about the economies that might be effected by the employment of this alphabet; to transliterate *Androcles and the Lion* into the new alphabet and publish it with "Dr. Johnson's

Alphabet" and the "Proposed British Alphabet" on opposite pages; and to present copies to public libraries throughout the world.

At the end of twenty-one years, or earlier if the purpose of the Will was then carried out, or earlier invalidated by judicial decision, the Residuary Estate was to be divided equally among the British Museum, the National Gallery of Ireland, and the Royal Academy of Dramatic Art.

Shaw's Will thus implemented his oft-proclaimed intentions. To carry out the provisions of the Will would have been a fitting denouement to the drama of GBS' life in which the protagonist had signified his life purposes in this regard many times. The continued growth of Shaw's estate after his death, attributable to the artistic and financial success of *My Fair Lady*, was poetic justice. The chances for effectuation of his plans were multiplied, should the returns be used for an improved English alphabet or language reform.

Lord Justice Charles Harman pointed out in his judicial decision concluding the litigation proceedings over Shaw's Will in 1957 that the Will "bears ample internal evidence of being in part the testator's own work." Those parts of the Will reproduced here seem to bear the Shavian stamp.

From the Will of Bernard Shaw
(1950)

Clause 35: "I devise and bequeath all my real and personal estate not otherwise specifically disposed of by this my will or any codicil hereto and all property over which I have general power of appointment unto my trustee upon trust that my trustee shall (subject to the power of postponing the sale and conversion thereof hereinafter contained) sell my real estate and sell call in or otherwise convert into money as much as may be needed of my personal estate (other than any copyrights which as provided by clause 7 of this my will are not to be sold) to increase the ready moneys of which I may be possessed at my death to an amount sufficient to pay my funeral and testamentary expenses and debts estate duty legacy duty and all the duties payable on my death in respect of my estate or the bequests hereby made free of duty (other than testamentary expenses) and the legacies bequeathed by this my will or any codicil hereto or to make such other payments or investments or charge of investments as in his opinion shall be advisable in the interest of my estate and shall invest the residue of such moneys in manner hereinafter authorized and shall stand possessed of the said residuary trust moneys and the investments for the time being representing the same and all other investments for the time being forming part of my residuary estate (herein called my residuary trust funds) and the annual income thereof upon the trusts hereby declared of and concerning the same: (1) To institute and finance a series of inquiries to ascertain or estimate as far as possible the following statistics (a) the number of extant persons who speak the English language and write it by the established and official alphabet of twenty-six letters (hereinafter called Dr. Johnson's alphabet); (b) how much time could be saved per individual scribe by the substitution for the said alphabet of an alphabet containing at least forty letters (hereinafter called the Proposed British alphabet) enabling the said language to be written without indicating single sounds by groups of letters or by diacritical marks, instead of by one symbol for each sound; (c) how many of these persons are engaged in writing or printing English at any and every moment in the world; (d) on these factors to estimate the time and labour wasted by our lack of at least fourteen unequivocal single symbols; (e) to add where possible to the estimates of time lost or saved by the difference between Dr. Johnson's alphabet and the Proposed British alphabet estimates of the loss of income in British and American currency. The inquiry must be confined strictly to the statistical and mathematical problems to be solved without regard to the views of professional and amateur phoneticians, etymologists, spelling reformers, patentees of universal languages, inventors of shorthand codes for verbatim reporting or rival alphabets, teachers of the established orthography, disputants about pronunciation, or of the irreconcilables whose wranglings have overlooked and confused the single issue of labour saving and made change impossible during the last hundred years. The inquiry must not imply any approval or disapproval of the Proposed British Alphabet by the inquirers or by my trustee. (2) To employ a phonetic expert to transliterate my play entitled *Androcles and the Lion* into the Proposed British alphabet assuming the pronunciation to resemble that recorded of His Majesty our late King George V and sometimes described as Northern English. (3) To employ an artist calligrapher to fair-copy the transliteration for reproduction by lithography photography or any other method that may serve in the absence of printers' types. (4) To advertise and publish the transliteration with the original

Dr. Johnson's lettering opposite the transliteration page by page and a glossary of the two alphabets at the end and to present copies to public libraries in the British Isles, the British Commonwealth, the American States North and South, and to national libraries everywhere in that order."

Clause 36: "I desire my trustee to bear in mind that the Proposed British Alphabet does not pretend to be exhaustive as it contains only sixteen vowels whereas by infinitesimal movements of the tongue countless different vowels can be produced all of them in use among speakers of English who utter the same vowel no oftener than they make the same fingerprints. Nevertheless they can understand one another's speech and writing sufficiently to converse and correspond."

Clause 37: "It is possible that the Ministry of Education may institute the inquiry and adopt the Proposed British alphabet to be taught in the schools it controls in which event subsection 1 of clause 35 foregoing and its relevant sequels will be contra-indicated as superfluous and clause 40 come into operation accordingly but the adoption must be exact and no account taken of the numerous alternative spelling reforms now advocated or hereafter proposed."

Clause 38: "I hereby devise and bequeath the balance of the income of my Residuary Trust Funds not required during the period of twenty-one years after my death to pay the annuities hereby or by my Codicil hereto bequeathed or for any other purpose upon which income of my Residuary Trust Funds may under the trusts hereinbefore contained be applicable upon trust during the special period but subject to cessor as hereinafter provided to apply the same as follows:—

A. To remunerate the services and defray the expenses incidental to these proceedings and generally to the launching advertising and propaganda of the said British alphabet.

B. To acquire by employment purchase or otherwise the copyrights and patents (if any) created by or involved in the designing and manufacture of the said Alphabet or the publication of the works printed in it without exploiting the said rights or for commercial profit.

C. To wind-up the enterprise when the aforesaid steps have been taken or if and when its official adoption or general vogue shall make further recourse to my estate and action on the part of my Trustee in respect of this charitable Trust superfluous."

The remaining sections of this anthology present writings about, rather than by, Shaw. The justification for their inclusion lies in their obvious relevance to a good understanding of the subject of this work.

"ON THE WILL OF BERNARD SHAW"

Excerpts from
Lord Justice Charles Harman's Decision, February, 1957

As has been aptly observed, "Where there's a Will, there's litigation." Even before GBS' Will was probated, *The New York Times* reported in December, 1950: "An unnamed defender of the English language has filed a court protest against the Will of George Bernard Shaw . . . He has petitioned the Probate Court to suspend probate of the Will on the ground that it 'gravely affects the majesty of the English language, and would have serious repercussions on English literature.'" Lady Astor, an old and close friend of Shaw's, termed the Will "ridiculous" when its provisions were revealed in 1951, adding that she could have better used the bequest herself.

Five years elapsed after GBS' death before any legal action commenced or any further public announcement was made about the fate of the Will. When the Public Trustee was apprised that there was doubt as to the legal validity of the Alphabet Trusts and that two of the residuary legatees, the British Museum and the Royal Academy, were contesting the Will, he called for a judicial construction. In accordance with British legal procedure, an Originating Summons was issued.

Lord (then Mr.) Justice Harman presided over the judicial proceedings of December, 1956 and January and February, 1957 that developed from the litigation over Shaw's Will. His decision was selected for inclusion in *The Law as Literature: An Anthology of Great Writing in and About the Law,* London, The Bodley Head, 1961. In the "Foreword" to that book, Lord Birkett said of the decision: "It is a perfect example of the blending of law and literature, and will hold its place in any company in any age." Editor Louis Blom-Cooper wrote: "It was almost inevitable that such a controversial figure in contemporary Britain as George Bernard Shaw should continue to provide argument and dispute even from his grave."

At the hearing, the Attorney General argued for the "Charity," i.e., the Alphabet Trust; the Public Trustee was neutral; and the three Residuary Legatees were named parties, although the National Gallery of Ireland "preferred to stand outside the controversy, not wishing to urge anything which would defeat the intention of a fellow-Irishman, and a very distinguished Irishman, in a matter which was clearly very dear to his heart." Mr. I. J. (now Sir James) Pitman, M.P., and Miss Barbara Smoker, then secretary of the Shaw Society of London, supported the cause of validating the Will, by offering data, research findings, and corroborative evidence to the Attorney General.

Miss Smoker has written that in her judgment, Justice Charles Harman's conduct of the trial was entirely fair and sympathetic to Shaw's intent. One of the judge's observations during the course of the trial suggested a pending judgment favorable to the Alphabet Trust, she thought. Mr. Justice Harman was reported to have said: "It was Mr. Shaw's money. Why should the law stop him?" The learned jurist went on to say of Shaw's complex testament: "It is ironic to think that perhaps the greatest master of language in this country has produced a document which has puzzled us for days, and I suppose will puzzle us some more."

The decision was rendered in February, 1957. The written judgment found that the Will did not create a valid charity. Hence, no part of Shaw's estate could legally be used to carry out his testamentary wishes concerning the Proposed British Alphabet, and the Residuary Legatees were to receive the bequest.

Editor Louis Blom-Cooper said, of Lord Justice Harman's decision: "Mr. Justice Harman, himself an Irishman, did justice in more senses than one to Shaw's literary merits. The judgment was not only a successful parody of Shaw's caustic and cynical style but a model of clarity."

Excerpts from "ON THE WILL OF BERNARD SHAW" by Lord Justice Harman, reprinted from *THE LAW AS LITERATURE* (1957)

All his long life Bernard Shaw was an indefatigable reformer. He was already well known when the present century dawned, as novelist, critic, pamphleteer, playwright, and during the ensuing half-century he continued to act as a kind of itching powder to the British public, to the English-speaking peoples, and, indeed to an even wider audience castigating their follies, their foibles and their fallacies, and bombarding them with a combination of paradox and wit that earned him in the course of years the status of an oracle: the Shavian oracle; and the rare distinction of adding a word to the language. Many of his projects he lived to see gain acceptance and carried into effect and become normal. It was natural that he should be interested in English orthography and pronunciation. These are obvious targets for the reformer. It is as difficult for the native to defend the one as it is for the foreigner to compass the other. The evidence shows that Shaw had for many years been interested in the subject. Perhaps his best known excursion in this field is *Pygmalion,* in which the protagonist is a professor of phonetics: this was produced as a play in 1914 and has held the stage ever since and invaded the world of the film. It is, indeed, a curious reflection that this same work, tagged with versicles which I suppose Shaw would have detested, and tricked out with music which he would have eschewed (see the preface to *The Admirable Bashville*), is now charming huge audiences on the other side of the Atlantic and has given birth to the present proceedings. I am told that the receipts from this source have enabled the executor to get on terms with the existing death duties payable on the estate, thus bringing the interpretation of the will into the realm of practical politics.

The testator, whatever his other qualifications, was the master of a pellucid style, and the reader embarks on his will confident of finding no difficulty in understanding the objects which the testator had in mind. This document, moreover, was evidently originally the work of a skilled equity draftsman. As such I doubt not it was easily to be understood if not of the vulgar at any rate by the initiate. Unfortunately the will bears ample internal evidence of being in part the testator's own work. The two styles, as ever, make an unfortunate mixture. It is always a marriage of incompatibles: the delicate testamentary machinery devised by the conveyancer can but suffer when subjected to the *cacoethes scribendi* of the author, even though the latter's language, if it stood alone, might be a literary masterpiece.

This will is a long and complicated document made on 12th June, 1950, when the testator was already ninety-four years old, though it is fair to say that it is rather youthful exuberance than the circumspection of old age that mars its symmetry.

I should have wished to regard this bequest as a gift

to the ultimate residuary legatees subject to a condition by which they cannot complain of income during the first twenty-one years after the testator's death being devoted to the alphabet project. This apparently might be the way in which the matter would be viewed in the United States. In my judgment, I am not at liberty to validate this trust by treating it as a power.

The result is that the alphabet trusts are, in my judgment, invalid, and must fail. It seems that their begotter suspected as much, hence his jibe about failure by judicial decision. I answer that it is not the fault of the law, but of the testator, who failed almost for the first time in his life to grasp the legal problem or to make up his mind what he wanted.

The writer of the Foreword and the following four pieces, Sir James Pitman, K.B.E., M.P., was a friend and collaborator of George Bernard Shaw. They engaged in lively correspondence, arising from their mutual respect and their common interest, but differing ideas, in the field of reform of the English language: its spelling and alphabet.

Shaw confided to Sir James his basic ideas and the plans for his Will. When Shaw's Will was in litigation, Sir James acted as advisor to the Solicitor General and the Public Trustee. The latter appointed Sir James a member of the committee which chose the winners of the "Proposed British Alphabet" contest stipulated in Shaw's Will.

COMMENTS ON THE DECISION IN RE SHAW'S WILL

by Sir James Pitman (1963)

The writer does not agree with the late Lord Birkett and so, by inference, disagrees also with Mr. Justice Harman. He believes that the very novelty of this field of thought (quite apart from the difficulties in linguistics in conveying meaning within what is a novel, indeed a revolutionary, field of thought consequently foreign to those who read such words only in their own habituated fields of thought) led to a misinterpretation of the adequately expressed intentions of Shaw in his Will.

It seems to the writer that the wording of Shaw's Will (if interpreted as English words should be interpreted in such a context) certainly set up a valid educational trust, and probably alternatively set up a limited and certain objective which, when carried out, would have been a once-and-for-all completion of a definite testamentary disposition—as much a valid testament as that in the famous precedent of the erection of a grave over the body of a surviving race horse.

To deal first with the second of these two points, the writer holds that this once-for-all completion of a finite memorial received insufficient argument. Moreover, it should have been argued by the Counsel for the Public Trustee, but was argued, at the request of the Judge, by Counsel for the Attorney General, who could not have been, and had not been, sufficiently informed and even, if at all, briefed, for this point of a once-for-all finite legacy of a memorial character. This point therefore would have been argued afresh by Counsel for the Public Trustee when the case went to the Court of Appeal, and might then have prevailed, had not those concerned agreed "as a compromise" to allow the Public Trustee to carry out the Will (as just such a memorial publication). It must, however, be conceded that, in this the second case, there was the absence of a wording to ensure that, if the memorial expenditure had not been concluded within twenty-one years, all further expenditure would need to cease. But this had been a provision which had been presumed in another case of a once-for-all memorial, where the maintenance of a surviving animal was involved—an animal which might, in fact, have extended the effective life of the Trust beyond the 21-year limiting period.

The other and earlier point—that the Alphabet Trust was valid as a charitable one, as well as a once-for-all finite Trust—would no doubt have been then argued also. It might indeed have been successfully argued, thus giving validity to the Will under one or other or both points. Indeed, there was much to support an argument that the Alphabet Trust was indeed a Charitable Trust, in that whereas a Trust such as to erect a grave over the body of a dead race horse could have little or indeed no public benefit, the intention of Shaw was to afford a general, and very great, public benefit. A project, such as building a bridge at a particular point, calculated to afford a limited public benefit, would have been not only legal, but warmly commended by the Courts. After all, research into the improving of education in, say, the fields of Mathematics or Science or Divinity, would presumably each have been held to be for the *advancement* of Education, and thus a valid basis for a charitable Trust. If Science and Divinity, why not reading and writing? Could there be any intention to advance Education more indubitably thus Educational, than to distribute copies of *Androcles and the Lion* free to Public Libraries, themselves a valid Charitable purpose, seeing that the ulterior purpose was also to advance education in the field of reading and writing?

It seemed to the writer that the climate in the Court was not only that Shaw's disposition could not be, and was not, of general public benefit, but that it was, if anything, contrary to public interest—so great is the emotionalism which surrounds all attempts to alter, even to query, the sacrosanctity of our established language conventions.

It seemed that, particularly in the second case, the words of the alphabet clauses were misinterpreted (because of the same question and the same novelty of the field of thought and the consequential inevitability of attributing to words meanings which have become habituated in other and quite different fields of thought) as implying not the finite disposition of a once-for-all action, but the continuing disposition which Harman J., I believe wrongly, held it to be. Perhaps the words "launching, advertising and propaganda" in Clause 38 tended to add difficulty further to the difficulties of this novel field of thought. To the writer this wording is wholly consistent with the finite enterprise of a publication of a book which Shaw described, and does not imply a continuing expenditure to persist in advertising and "propagandizing" an alphabetic system in which a book so "launched" had been printed. The writer is a publisher (as Shaw incidentally also was, and was requiring the Public Trustee to be) and the word "propaganda" in such a publishing context clearly refers (in contra-distinction to any advertisement for designers, calligraphers, etc.) to the copies (some 13,000 it has been) which were to be distributed free to Public and National libraries as a particularised propaganda effect. In my view, Clause 38 is thus clearly confined to the payment for the costs which would arise from the once-for-all publication of a particular book—and for nothing else.

With the present success of Pitman's I.T.M., perhaps the obscurantism which quite unconsciously must always be present among Judges, as amongst all of their environment, would now be less. The concept that "interfering" with our literary heritage could be of general public benefit might, in consequence of what has been demonstrated in the experimental classes, be now conceded and no longer be instinctively and contemptuously resisted. Perhaps with all of this the educational character of the project would have been, if grudgingly, appreciated.

Perhaps, too, with the publication and "propaganda" distribution of 13,000 copies of *Androcles* to Public Libraries, the true intention and better interpretation of the alphabet clauses might now be more easily explained.

Certainly at the time it was, as events have shown, impossible for the writer adequately to "educate" Counsel in such novel fields of thought, and thus to have put to the Court, with any hope of acceptance, the view that Shaw's words meant what they said they meant. Perhaps it would now be clear that the decision against Shaw came about, not because Shaw's meaning was not clear and a valid disposition, but because those reading them were out of tune with the field of thought into which it was necessary to enter in order to interpret it.

A reader needs to be attuned to the field of thought of musicians or else he will be led astray by such words as "color," "meaning," "movement," etc. which have no semblance of meaning as interpreted in all other fields of human thought. A Judge from Mars, knowing nothing of music, would be hard put to it to give a decision based upon the interpretation of such words present in a disputed Will. In this field of attempted "education" of Counsel in a new field of thought, the writer was by no means welcomed, much less assisted by "The Establishment." The Public Trustee and the Attorney General's Learned Counsel were very receptive and desirous of learning, but such preferred collaboration was not so cordially welcomed in higher circles, as may be judged from the culminating occasion when, in the matter of possible appeal to the Court of Appeal, access to such Counsel was refused at the direction of the Attorney General (see the writer's statement to the Press dated 5th March, *The Times* of

6th March, and Hansard of 7th May 1957), and this in a context in which, as it turned out, the grounds for such an appeal were regarded as sufficient to merit the "compromise" which enabled the Public Trustee to carry out the Will, thus vindicating to some effective degree one or both of the contentions that the Trust had been a Charitable one and/or that a once-for-all memorial publication had been what the terms of the Will had intended and expressed.

However, it does not any longer matter. Shaw's Will has now been carried out as he intended. The statistical survey which was to show the "money value" of a better alphabet may yet be carried out and this, together with the savings demonstrated by the juxtaposition of the Roman and the Shaw, may give a later opportunity to point the value of a new non-romanic alphabet designed to supplement our three present romanic ones—upper case, lower case and cursive.

It is possible that the English-speaking peoples will not forever tolerate that their *only* form of written communication should be the one which was used by the Romans for the laborious carving in stone to commemorate in perpetuity the victories of their Emperors—a form which had been conceived, designed and evolved with disregard of speed and convenience in conveying meaning. It is possible that Shaw's concept and Isaac Pitman's concept—that a modern civilized community which daily covers many thousands of acres of clean white paper with written communications, would one day evolve an alternative form—will come about. Until then it is well to remind ourselves that we spend at least six times as much time and effort in any written as in the corresponding spoken communication, essentially because the former form was designed for the most "tedious, cumbrous and wearisome" imaginable execution, whilst the latter has been evolved to be as "rapid, easy and delightful" as possible.

"MY FAIR LADIES—AND GENTLEMEN"

by Sir James Pitman

An Insert in theatre programs (1958)

Sir James wrote "My Fair Ladies—and Gentlemen," a commentary distributed in the playbills at the London production of *My Fair Lady* in 1958-9, in which the story of Shaw's interest in alphabet and spelling reform was told.

Sir James pursued his spelling reform convictions for many years as Treasurer of the Simplified Spelling Society of Great Britain, whose program he supported in prolific writing and lecturing, and in the Commons debates over spelling reform legislation in 1949 and 1953. He also heads Sir Isaac Pitman and Sons, the printing establishment that bears the name of his famous grandfather, founder of the Pitman shorthand system and a spelling reformer and phonetician in his own time.

My Fair Ladies — and Gentlemen

by Sir James Pitman

Shaw's interest in speech—shall we say pronunciation —and in its importance, was the origin of "My Fair Lady." Thanks to the musical version of "Pygmalion" this human problem has come to be widely recognized.

But what is not yet so widely recognized is the conclusion which Shaw was intending to teach—that our present form of written communication makes good speech more difficult, and that a better form could be introduced.

Shaw's point was that it is wrong that our written language does not, and—lacking 17 of the 40 necessary letters—cannot, reflect The Queen's English or any other version of English.

In his Will he provided for the design of a British alphabet *additional to our Roman alphabet*—an alphabet of 40 letters at least, in which one visible letter, and only one, was to represent one audible letter. He objected to SH, wanting one new letter in lieu of the combination of two quite irrelevant old letters. He objected also to H h (which are two very different versions of but a single letter), insisting on only one form for any letter. Indeed, he wanted to get right away from the 26 Roman letters to a newly-to-be-designed set of 40 British letters.

In Shaw's view, WOZ for WAS is, and always will be, an "obscenity." Therefore the new alphabet, if it were to be acceptable, must have brand new forms for W, for O, and for Z,—in which case the new word-form for WAS would become a form both so new and so economical that everyone might see without prejudice the advantage of the new form.

No wonder that he expected that his Will would be opposed in the Courts. It was. However by agreement of the British Museum, the Royal Academy of Dramatic Art and the National Gallery of Ireland (whose generous attitude I am pleased to be able to acknowledge) Shaw's Will is to be carried out in full.

The money is thus available to design the "Proposed British Alphabet" and to print his play "Androcles and the Lion" with one page in the new alphabet (in a "pronunciation to resemble that recorded of His Majesty our late King George V") in contrast to the other in the present Roman alphabet and spelling. With the aid of a "glossary" of the new letters, and the "crib" of parallel pages, any intelligent reader of English, as now printed, ought to be able, after but a few hours of intensive study, to read—if haltingly—in the new alphabet.

Copies of the book are then, under the Will, to be given to every public library in the English-speaking world, and every national library in every other country.

At the same time an investigation into the amount of writing and printing of the English language will be undertaken and an estimate made of the yearly savings (expressed in $ as well as in £) which may be expected in using his Proposed British Alphabet.

Shaw's intention was to do for *Roman letters* what the *new Arabic system* had *already* done for *Roman numerals*—give a better alternative which could be added to their repertoire by those intelligent enough to appreciate its advantages. "VI" is less good than "6" as a means of representing the number which follows "five." More than one sign (a "one" and a "vee") is inevitable in Roman numerals because there are less than ten units of symbolization with which to represent the ten units of numbering. Similarly, the four signs "SHAW" afford a poor way of representing the two units of the author's name. Four signs are necessary because with only 26 letters for 40 units of sound there is no letter for ISH and no letter for AU. In the Proposed British Alphabet there will be two such letters. But Shaw's two-letter form is not intended to drive out our present four-letter SHAW. After all, the later and different *s*, h, a, and *a* have not driven out the original S, H, and A, nor "6" driven out "VI." The choice is made to suit the purpose.

The number of written letters per word will be considerably reduced. Moreover, such fewer letters could occupy less space than do the present letters—for instance, W, M, H take up an unnecessary width in the line of printing. It is likely, then, that Shaw's Alphabet will yield at least a reduction in space occupied as did the introduction of the new Arabic numerals "1958" alternative to the Roman "MCMLVIII."

The amount of printing and writing done every second of the day and night in the world, and of paper, ink, machine-time, storage and transport is so great that savings of £3,000,000 or $10,000,000 *a day* will be eventually possible. Meanwhile, a prize of £500 is offered by the Public Trustee for such an alphabet: and designs are being submitted by men and women from all parts of the world.

Shaw was indeed not unintelligent—rather was he insufficiently understood. Many of his ideas were so novel and so penetrating that they were rejected by his contemporaries—and this particular idea was so novel, and so demanding in its need to think freshly, that very few people have yet understood it.

In effect, he wants the Eliza Doolittles (and the Higginses) to have a good modern alphabet placed at their disposal. If they find it easy to learn (and far better to use) they will not only save themselves time and money, but those who need to will come to recognize at once—because sight will supplement hearing—in precisely what the *"Rhine in Spine"* differs from the *"Rain in Spain."*

"Androcles and the Lion" in this most interesting format will be published probably late in 1959: please keep a space in your bookshelf for it, and above all, do not allow any adverse predisposition, with which you may have started, to becloud your judgment of a great Irishman, or of his last Will and Testament which generously and ingeniously sought to achieve for the language he so greatly loved the dearly cherished hopes of an exceptional man.

P.S. Shaw used Pitman's shorthand for all his writings, but he realized that a system designed for quick writing could not also be best for everyday reading. He nevertheless appreciated that my grandfather's system had already and widely proved three of his points:

1. That a 40-letter alphabet does indeed succeed for English.
2. That a new word-form alternative to our present longhand is indeed acceptable—for it quickly spread all round the world.
3. That literally anyone who really wishes to learn a new alphabet will be able to do so—and will do so.

"INTRODUCTION TO SHAW'S ALPHABET," from *The Shaw Alphabet Edition of Androcles and the Lion* (1962) by Sir James Pitman

An appeal was taken from Justice Harman's decision over the GBS Will, as urged by Sir James Pitman and Miss Barbara Smoker. However, the legal tangle was resolved in December, 1957. The Court of Appeals accepted an out-of-court compromise among the disputants to carry out substantially the alphabet trusts provided in Shaw's Will. The Public Trustee was permitted to spend £8,300 for the purposes, by agreement with the Residuary Legatees.

Accordingly, a prize of £500 was offered in 1958 in a contest to select a "Proposed British Alphabet" of at least 40 symbols. Four contestants out of 467 entrants were declared the joint winners. A composite alphabet was developed by Kingsley Read, and the transliteration of *Androcles and the Lion* by Peter MacCarthy of the Department of Phonetics at Leeds University has been printed in the special *Shaw Alphabet Edition.* 3500 copies of the book have been "given to every public library in the English-speaking world and every national library in every other country," as required by Shaw's bequest, said Public Trustee C. R. Sopwith in the Foreword to the book (Penguin Books, 1962).

The *Shaw Alphabet Edition* of *Androcles and the Lion* was published in accordance with the compromise that ended the litigation over Shaw's Will. C. R. Sopwith, the Public Trustee, dedicated that book "to Sir James Pitman K.B.E. M.P. in grateful acknowledgement of his unstinted co-operation and continuous support over a period of nine years in carrying out Bernard Shaw's wishes."

Sir James wrote for the *Shaw Alphabet Edition* an "Introduction to Shaw's Alphabet," which is here reproduced.

INTRODUCTION TO SHAW'S ALPHABET

by Sir James Pitman

(*Shaw Alphabet Edition of Androcles and the Lion,* 1962)

Here is Shaw's alphabet. It has been proved that those who wish to read it can do so after only a few hours of concentrated deciphering.

Why should anyone wish to use it? And why should there be any departure from the familiar forms of the Roman alphabet in which English is printed and written?

You will notice from the comparisons that Shaw's alphabet is both more legible and one-third more economical in space than traditional printing, and this should lead to a great increase in reading speed. The characters themselves are very distinct. To prove them more legible, open the book and hold it upside down in front of a mirror. Both mirrored pages will thus become equally unfamiliar. Keep the back of the book pressed against your lips, and advance towards the mirror until you are able to see individual characters clearly enough to be able to copy them. Note that the Shaw characters are clearly seen at a greater distance.

The economy in space and greater simplicity of characters ought also to increase the speed and ease of *writing*—even more than it does the ease of reading. Many of the characters easily join into pairs and trios to form syllables which recur frequently in English words; the sounds of the language are completely characterized, thus permitting abbreviation with great reliability. Shaw found traditional script too laborious, and Pitman's shorthand too economical. Though at this time we can only guess, it is probable that an abbreviated handwriting speed of 60-100 words a minute, with complete reliability of reading, will be possible for those who attain 'automatic' facility with Shaw's alphabet. In other words, reading may be 50-75 per cent, and writing 80-100 per cent faster, and even 200-300 per cent, by using simple abbreviations.

Shaw insisted that, unless his alphabet were to offer the substantial advantages he himself desired, there would be no reason for adding to the existing media of communication, which include: typewriting, shorthand, morse, semaphore, and braille, in addition to the Roman alphabet which is itself represented by three quite different sets of signs (as in 'ALPHABET,' 'alphabet,' and '*alphabet*').

The Key on page 151 (duplicated on the bookmark) will enable you to achieve the beginnings of skill and the satisfaction of success within three or four hours. Although this means starting from scratch, remember that Isaac Pitman, whose shorthand Shaw used for all his writings, also did so with a system offering the same advantages as Shaw's alphabet: that is, the saving of time, effort, and money.

Shaw did not want you and me to *abandon* the Roman alphabet. The long-established Roman figures (I, II, III, IV, V, VI, VII, VIII, IX) remain even after the Arabic figures (the newer and handier 0, 1, 2, 3, 4, 5, 6, 7, 8, 9) have found favour. We now use both with greater convenience. The new figures were not imposed, nor the old supplanted. Similarly, Shaw believed, uses would be found for a new and handier alphabet *without* abandoning the old one.

If those who tried it found it advantageous, they would use it, and by their example it would gain what following it deserved. If its benefits were substantial enough, it would spread and establish itself through merit—as Arabic numerals did despite the then complete satisfaction with Roman numerals.

Utilitarian advantage is thus the principle governing the new alphabet. Shaw was unique in pointing out that substantial economy could be attained only (*a*) if the designer were to *depart* from a system evolved by the Romans 2,000 years ago for carving their public notices in stone; (*b*) if a single set of alphabetical characters were used—abolishing the different look of words in capitals, small letters, and linked handwritten letters; and (*c*) if each distinct sound of the language were spelt with its own unvarying character.

These three factors in designing, taken together, made a non-Roman alphabet essential. Of course, there is nothing revolutionary in that. There are hundreds of non-Roman alphabets—and there are several variations within the Roman alphabet, e.g.

Roman variations	HERE IS A SENTENCE here is a sentence *here is a sentence*
Russian	ир ис а сентенс
Greek	ἡρ ις α σεντενς

Thus these four *English* words may already be represented in a number of existing alphabets.

Those who know Greek and English, Russian and English, etc., will have no difficulty in reading that sentence immediately in as many alphabets as they know—and it is considered at school that once a child has learned his A, B, C, D he is well placed to learn also his a, b, c, d, his *a, b, c, d,* his α, β, γ, δ (Greek) and his а, б, в, г (Russian).

Only a few hours will be needed to persuade you that the new alphabet has the potential advantages Shaw intended for it. At first you will read and write it in a plodding childlike way, as you once did Roman. Much more rapidly than a child's, your familiarity and ease will grow, until the use of Shaw's alphabet becomes as natural and automatic as your use of Roman—but faster.

In personal and intimate writing the forty-eight (40+8) characters of the Shaw alphabet may faithfully portray the pronunciation of the individual; but, as Shaw pointed out, too eccentric a dialect may hamper, and even destroy, effective communication. He considered that, though there was no need to standardize writing if not intended for publication, there was every need for conformity in print; standard spellings being particularly desirable when that print is intended for circulation throughout the English-speaking world.

In his Will, Shaw specified just such a standardization for this play. He laid down for it a 'pronunciation to resemble that recorded of His Majesty our late King George V and sometimes described as Northern English.' He was an expert in stage direction and, so it may be supposed, considered this pronunciation to be the best basis for comprehension with acceptability in reading as he had found it to be in speech from the stage.

But by all means *write* as you think fit, and leave experts to standardize printers' spelling.

This book costs very little. Get your friends to buy one and to learn the alphabet so that you can write to one another—or, if you become so skilled that you no longer need to 'keep your eye in,' give it away.

JAMES PITMAN

House of Commons
London
1962

NOTE: I have offered, if there is the demand, to organize what were known as 'ever-circulators' in the early days of my grandfather. Send me a letter in Shaw's alphabet, mentioning your particular interests or circumstances. Give me your name and address in ordinary writing on an enclosed envelope. I will then try to arrange 'circles' of five or six who, drawn together in a friendship by Shaw's alphabet, will all circulate their own letters to which each in turn will add.

I have also offered, if there is a demand, to get further material published in the Shaw alphabet. When you have learnt to read and write fluently, and want more than your ever-circulator correspondence to read, please write to me, Sir James Pitman, K.B.E., M.P., at the House of Commons, London S.W. 1, England, saying which of Shaw's works or other literature you would like to read in a printed transcription. I can make no promises—other than to consider your suggestions most sympathetically. Meanwhile, if anyone wishes to get printed their own material in Shaw's alphabet, they are permitted to do so, since the copyright for the alphabet and for the type-faces is public property. Messrs. Stephen Austin & Sons, Ltd., of Caxton Hill, Ware Road, Hertford, England, hold a supply of the types and are willing to undertake the work. For the moment, type available is confined to 12-point size in the three founts exemplified in this book.

* * *

ON THE SHAW AND INITIAL TEACHING ALPHABETS

by Sir James Pitman (1963)

Sir James Pitman is the moving spirit in an important experiment in teaching British school children to read, begun in September, 1961 and carried on by a committee of the National Foundation for Educational Research in England and Wales. In this study, children learn to read English by use of a transitional Initial Teaching Alphabet, from which they later transfer to traditional orthography. As a result of Sir James' visits to America, and his lectures and writings and those of John Downing, similar researches are taking shape in America. Shaw's writings have had some effect, too, in promoting interest in such efforts, especially those of Dr. Godfrey Dewey of the Simpler Spelling Association.

These developments are somewhat at variance with the purposes of GBS. Sir James' purpose is to help English speaking beginners to learn to read more easily, and those who know only other languages to learn to speak and read English with greater facility. GBS' purpose was to help those who read and write in the present orthography to become more efficient readers and writers in a new alphabet, which would eventually replace the present one because of its relative, competitive efficiency.

Sir James' purpose is to preserve all that is alphabetic in our present Roman orthography; GBS wished to depart altogether from the defects and handicaps of the Roman alphabet.

In the essay, "On the Shaw And Initial Teaching Alphabets,"

written especially for this volume, Sir James explains how his work differs rather fundamentally from that of Shaw, though they shared the common objective of lifting the alphabetic burden to free the mind of man—and child.

ON THE SHAW AND INITIAL TEACHING ALPHABETS

By Sir James Pitman

(1963)

Those reading this interesting and illuminating work should appreciate wherein George Bernard Shaw and I differed and wherein we agreed.

Otherwise there will be confusion, since the Initial Teaching Alphabet which I have proposed has attracted at least as much attention as the new non-romanic alphabet which was proposed by G.B.S. in his Will and has recently been published.

Indeed so apt is the public to equate all changes from our traditional orthography, however different, that such confusion has been rife.

Fortunately, the recent publication of the Shaw Alphabet Edition of *Androcles and the Lion*, in paperback by Penguin Books, shows the text printed in parallel page form; the traditional orthographic page being a line for line key to the Shaw alphabet page. There is a bookmark, too, which contains what G.B.S. called a "glossary"—that is to say, a character to character key.

It is possible, therefore, to convey the distinction and to reduce confusion by a concrete rather than, as necessary hitherto, only an abstract explanation.

Here, then, are specimens of the two alphabets reproducing the opening sentence of this statement.

thœz reediŋ this interestiŋ and illueminætiŋ wurk ʃhood appreeʃhiæt whærin jorj bernard ʃhau and ie differd and whærin wee agreed.

𐑞𐑴𐑟 𐑮𐑰𐑛𐑦𐑙 𐑞𐑦𐑕 𐑦𐑯𐑑𐑼𐑧𐑕𐑑𐑦𐑙 𐑯 𐑦𐑤𐑵𐑥𐑦𐑯𐑱𐑑𐑦𐑙 𐑢𐑻𐑒 𐑖𐑫𐑛 𐑩𐑐𐑮𐑰𐑖𐑦𐑱𐑑
𐑢𐑺𐑮𐑦𐑯 ·𐑡𐑹𐑡 𐑚𐑻𐑯𐑼𐑛 𐑖𐑷 𐑯 𐑲 𐑛𐑦𐑓𐑼𐑛 𐑯 𐑢𐑺𐑮𐑦𐑯 𐑢𐑰 𐑩𐑜𐑮𐑰𐑛.

Several points will be immediately apparent.

1. The former, the Augmented Roman (the writer's Initial Teaching Alphabet or I.T.A.), is Romanic.

2. It (the writer's Initial Teaching Alphabet—I.T.A.) is designed as an interim medium leading to a reading skill in the romanic Final Medium (F.M.) to which the child must and will make a transition.

3. It is unsuitable for those who already have a habituated reading skill in the F.M., our present roman alphabet. It in no way improves, indeed, at least at the outset, it reduces the ease of reading; it would greatly reduce, indeed it would overthrow the writing (i.e. spelling) skill of literates in the English language were they to wish (which they do not) to abandon the final medium and to write only in the I.T.A.

4. It is, however, highly compatible with the forms to which such literates have habituated themselves and in consequence, as has been found in current experimental classes in Britain, children find it easy, having learnt to read and write in the I.T.A., to habituate themselves thereafter to the reading and writing of the traditional orthographic forms of the F.M.

Per contra, the Shaw Alphabet is seen to be

1. Non-Romanic

2. Designed in no way for the purpose of teaching reading or writing *in the present Romanic media.*

3. It is, however, designed to afford, to those already (necessarily or they would not be adequately educated) habituated in the traditional orthography (T.O.), the opportunities of faster reading and faster writing of the English language. (It is to be noted that inevitable in such a design is the opportunity of economy also in time taken in composing and typing in areas of paper, of printing surfaces, of book shelves.)

4. It is in no way compatible with the traditional orthography and requires any such literate to learn two media—the Roman and the Shaw—just as he has learnt two media for numeration, the roman M C M L X III & 1963. (It is to be noted that the learning of an alternative medium imposes only an insignificant

burden on the already literate, or how else have we come to learn "bag" in a newer medium as an alternative for B A G in the old—and original—romanic medium?)

In my conversations and correspondence with Shaw, it took me a very long time to grasp the contrasts and the quite different benefits—and beneficiaries—of our respective intentions.

I had tried hard to persuade G.B.S. that there was a crying need with the continuation of the old Roman characters to teach Johnny how to read, and to make English a world language, by ensuring that in learning to read, those to whom English was a new tongue would be helped instead of grossly misled (cf. "stove," "move," "mauve," or even "go," "no," "so," "do," "who," "to") and in preserving English from splitting, as Latin did, into Italian, Spanish, Portuguese, etc.

He blessed my intentions, accepted the desirability and agreed with my analysis, but he regarded the English speaking world as impermeable to logic and to reason, or even self interest. He was certain that the "Establishment," in the New World and the Dominions as much as in conservative England, would fight to the death and never yield. He knew his history and was certain that to seek to change even one word, much less Teddy Roosevelt's 300 words, would bring all the most powerful hornets of the land around the head of any suicidal innovator. He bluntly asked whether my own career had been helped by such association, in the eyes of the Establishment, with those who scribbled obscene pencillings in public lavatories. How did even the man in the street, quite apart from Cabinet Ministers and University Chancellors and Presidents, view "woz" instead of "was?" They had learnt that while "has" spells "haz," "was" spells not "waz" but "woz" and regarded then their very own success in mastering such difficulties and their determination to continue them as the entrenchment of their superiority—and the symbol of their status.

With his smiling eyes and Irish brogue, he charmingly reminded me that my grandfather had been one of the world's truly great men, that he had worked all his long life as few men in their generation are able to work, that he had given every penny he made from his phonetic shorthand to phonetic longhand. He reeled off the names of the other great workers, all those named by Dr. Tauber (in his history of spelling reformers). In a situation where *all* had failed, how could the writer hope to succeed? The task had become, moreover, even more difficult as more and more vested interests became entrenched.

Only benefit in use would afford the key in a world which was against change. To my pleas that while I accepted the logic that those already literate would not gain benefit but would need to face disturbance, it was nevertheless worth accepting the disadvantages of such a change to benefit young children, some 25-30% of whom out of each age group failed to become adequately literate. The reply was that children had no votes and could not write to *The Times* as their adversaries would, and that in any case we must not be sentimental about those who so failed. The really constructive work in each generation was done by .001% of each age group and that such men and women had no difficulty in becoming literate and in playing their full part in the drama of human progress.

The next day I received one of his famous postcards:

> I said that the first thing to be provided is an alfabet. But this is not enough. The schools cannot experiment until we provide them with a primer with reading and writing exercises. I am half inclined to draft it myself.
> Meanwhile write up in letters of gold round your office *England Knows Nothing of Phonetics, Hates Education, But Will Do Anything For Money.*

I for my part had accepted the logic of the case for a non-romanic alphabet. Indeed, I would be the last man to be able to refute it in the light of his further argument based on my grandfather's experience.

I thus accepted Shaw's point that an alphabet evolved over two thousand years ago for the purpose of display in Rome on triumphal arches glorifying Roman Emperors, not in English but in Latin, was no starting point for a designer of a new alphabet. I accepted, too, that what I was proposing was the mere alphabetic use in the initial teaching stage only of what was a prehistoric legacy. I was not proposing it as an improved functional tool for reading and writing once those skills had been acquired. I accepted, too, that only by jettisoning our present prehistoric tool would it be possible to answer the fundamental question which I found that he well remembered, that my grandfather had posed in one of the earliest editions (1842) of his *Introduction to Phonography*. Why is that, in respect of *spoken* and *written* communication, "Hitherto, among all nations, there has existed the greatest disparity, in point of facility and dispatch, between these two methods of communication: the former has always been comparatively rapid, easy, and delightful; the latter, tedious, cumbrous, and wearisome. It is most strange that we, who excel our progenitors so far, in science, literature, and commerce, should continue to use a mode of writing, which, by its complexity, obliges the readiest hand to spend at least *six* hours in writing what can be spoken in *one*. Why do we use a long series of arbitrary marks to represent what the voice utters at a single effort? Why, in short, are not our *written signs* as simple as our *spoken sounds*? It cannot be said that this is impracticable . . ."

Above all I accepted the unanswerability of his two-fold question. "How is it that of the two great works of your grandfather, that which departs totally from the roman alphabet and imposes not only a greater but a considerable burden on the learner, spread like wild-fire from the pen of a penurious schoolmaster in a remote village in Gloucestershire throughout the whole English speaking world? Whereas the other, which was so romanic as to be immediately legible, was stillborn—had no breath in it despite the ceaseless efforts of great devoted adherents to inspire its inert corpse? Why did I, G.B.S., spend many hours learning Isaac's shorthand, and why do I now write all my plays and indeed all my works in it and yet use not at all his phonetic longhand which is so simple to learn—and so useless in practice?!"

He was respectfully handling the Bible in "The Great Isaac's" phonetic longhand but rejected its characterization and all other romanic systems. It was of no interest to him and he was excluding from his Will it and any and every other alphabet which, because it would be seeking continuity with the handicap which we had inherited, could *never* achieve the benefits in use which a designer having no such restrictions and limitations from the past, might achieve. He was not expecting anything as complicated and as fast as Pitman's shorthand. That was too fast. Any alphabet writing system which could keep pace, as the great Isaac's, with the winged words of the fastest speakers *must*, he claimed, be too complex for his purposes or it could not achieve such apparent miracles. He was therefore excluding from eligibility, under the Will (clause 35(1)) "the views of professional and amateur phoneticians, etymologists, Spelling Reformers, patentees of universal languages, inventors of shorthand codes for verbatim reporting or rival alphabets, teachers of the established orthography, disputants about pronunciation, or any of the irreconcilables whose wranglings have overlooked and confused the single issue of labour saving and made change impossible during the last hundred years."

I, in turn, blessed his intentions, accepted the desirability and agreed with his analysis, but I, in turn, took leave to doubt its practicality, and to turn on him his very arguments that the English speaking world is not logical and might well reject an "outlandish" alphabet which would be likened to Arabic or Devenagari.

Each was sympathetic and agreeable with the other—and not only on the main point in common (that of awareness of the inefficiency of the roman alphabet and of its present English orthography), but also on all the points other than the respective degrees of very great practical difficulty, if not impracticality, of hoping to win acceptance. The writer maintained that granted the money, it would be possible to demonstrate the superiority in teaching illiterates to read our present romanic orthography through a truly alphabetic romanic medium which, by augmenting the present roman alphabet, would enable the roman alphabet to be taught alphabetically. I expressed the belief that political pressures would then ensure that young children would no longer be handicapped by the obscurantism of the already literate; Shaw maintained that when his Will came to be carried out, the time saving and convenience of an efficient new alphabet would be so clearly demonstrated that teaching would take place first with a new alphabet and the old relegated to a secondary position. G.B.S. was interesting in his reason for leaving to a high functionary in the British Civil Service (The Public Trustee) and to the "sacrosanctity" of testamentary provisions, the formulation of his fresh set of conventions. He refused to set himself up as an authority on the grounds that no one would or should take from him ex cathedra decisions as to the shape and allocation of any new characters, which would need to become as unquestionable as our present A a B b etc. It was, he said, enough for him to lay down a requirement (clause 35(1)) of "at least 40 letters (hereinafter called the Proposed British Alphabet) enabling the said language to be written without indicating single sounds by groups of letters or by diacritical marks instead of by one symbol for each sound" for the new alphabet, and to require the Public Trustee so to determine.

If he laid down, even in the Will, the details of what new characters were to be used, it would touch off arguments even more heated than his Will and that if the Will—argumentative as it would be, were to be carried out, there would be no argument about detail, only argument about whether to use the alphabet when made available or not. That would be settled by those who tested it and would either find it better served their purposes than either longhand or even shorthand, or that it did not. If the benefit in use were enough, it would spread as Arabic numerals spread. He was forcing no one—only affording an opportunity. If it "flopped," perhaps someone later might have a better idea, or a better timing; he could do no more than lay a trough of water before the horse and he was determined to do that. He had made his Will and he stood by it. Let the Public Trustee do his best; all such issues would be settled when he was dead and cremated.

Meanwhile, the inquisitive public has found that much of what Shaw claimed was right: what the writer and many others have already found, that a new and non-romanic alphabet may be rapidly learned and expectations to the contrary are ill founded and false.

Such agreement in two such apparently conflicting approaches was most cordial—because the element of disagreement was solely on the relative weight of difficulty to be overcome. Each wished the other success—each wished a double success, because even when the Shaw alphabet becomes as prevalent an alternative to roman as roman lower case is to upper case that is to say as a to A, and the italic *a* to both (a to A and *a*), there will still be need to acquire alternative reading skills in those three romanic alphabets and in those present spellings with them which constitute our present traditional orthography.

G.B.S. support in *The Times* for reform and even for the teaching reform of an I.T.A. has been very valuable. He asked the writer to support his Will and that the writer may claim that he has done, to the extent that it is definite that without that support there would not now be any Shaw Alphabet as he had willed it.

The Shaw Alphabet for Writers

Double lines ⁚ between pairs show the relative height of Talls, Deeps, and Shorts. Wherever possible, finish letters rightwards; those starred * will be written upwards. Also see heading and footnotes overleaf.

	Tall		Deep				Short		Short	
peep	𐑐	:	𐑚	bib		if	𐑦	:	𐑰	eat
tot	𐑑	:	𐑛	dead		egg	𐑧	:	𐑱	age
kick	𐑒	:	𐑜	gag		ash*	𐑨	:	𐑲	ice
fee	𐑓	:	𐑝	vow		ado*	𐑩	:	𐑳	up
thigh	𐑔	:	𐑞	they		on	𐑪	:	𐑴	oak
so	𐑕	:	𐑟	zoo		wool	𐑫	:	𐑵	ooze
sure	𐑖	:	𐑠	meaSure		out	𐑬	:	𐑶	oil
church	𐑗	:	𐑡	judge		ah*	𐑭	:	𐑷	awe
yea	𐑘	:	𐑢	*woe		are	𐑸	:	𐑹	or
hung	𐑙	:	𐑣	ha-ha		air	𐑺	:	𐑻	err
	Short		Short			array	𐑼	:	𐑽	ear
loll	𐑤	:	𐑮	roar					Tall	
mime*	𐑥	:	𐑯	nun		Ian	𐑾	:	𐑿	yew

From *The Shaw Alphabet Edition of Androcles and the Lion* (Penguin Books 1962)

The Shaw Alphabet Reading Key

The letters are classified as Tall, Deep, Short, and Compound.
Beneath each letter is its full name: its *sound* is shown in **bold** type.

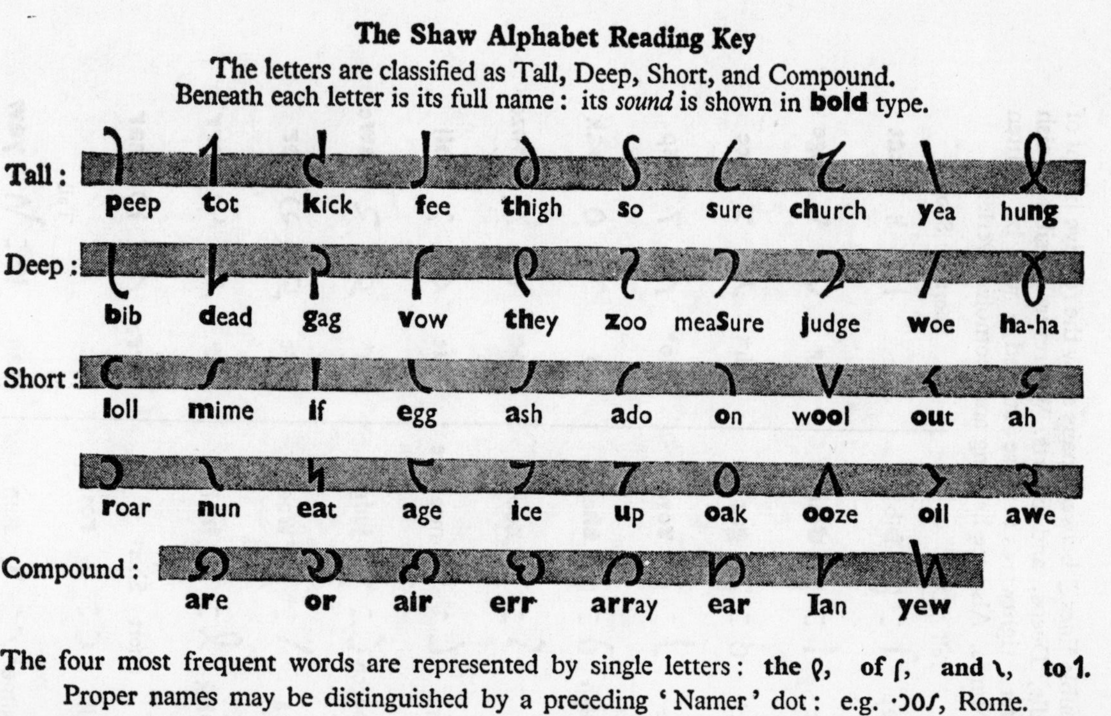

The four most frequent words are represented by single letters: **the** 𐑞, **of** 𐑝, **and** 𐑯, **to** 𐑑.
Proper names may be distinguished by a preceding 'Namer' dot: e.g. ·𐑮𐑴𐑥, Rome.
Punctuation and numerals are unchanged. Learn the alphabet *in pairs*, as listed for Writers overleaf.

From *The Shaw Alphabet Edition of Androcles and the Lion*
(Penguin Books 1962)

EPILOGUE

So even if GBS' Will is not being carried out in every detail, his will is. Shaw's serious concern for improving the language by lifting the alphabetical burden may at last get the chance he hoped and worked for. The direction and purpose he pointed to and expressed so often and so well in his writings are being carried on.

INDEX